"*The Alchemy of Talent by Dr. Vijay Pendakur offers a clear and insightful exploration of team dynamics and leadership. This approachable, science-based guide provides a practical perspective on leading teams through uncertainty. Pendakur skillfully reframes the value of diversity and inclusion to address today's challenges, focusing on performance science rather than the noise of polarization. His simple and effective model for optimizing the employee experience ensures that teams can consistently perform at their best. Enriched with actionable strategies, this book equips leaders with the tools to nurture resilience and foster innovation, making it an essential read for modern leadership.*"

—**DR. KARIE WILLYERD,** six-time Chief Learning Officer, and bestselling author of *The 2020 Workplace* and *Stretch: How to Futureproof Yourself*

"*World-class teams make world-class companies. The Alchemy of Talent is purpose-built for leading teams through the multitude of challenges all teams face. For any leader who wants their teams to do the best work in their lives, this book is a must-read.*"

—**JIM REID,** former Chief Human Resources Officer, Rogers Communications, and author of *Leading to Greatness*

"Team leaders and managers need simple, impactful, and clear guidance to handle disruption, achieve results, and empower the connectivity of their teams. The Alchemy of Talent provides a fresh, accessible view of how one can immediately take action with science-based techniques."

—**MICHAEL OHATA,** former Talent Leader and Chief Learning Officer, KPMG LLP, and author of *The Talent-Fueled Enterprise*

"Teams in higher education face ongoing volatility and uncertainty. The Alchemy of Talent is a clear, practical, evidence-driven guide that can help leaders support and empower their teams to not just survive today's challenging academic landscape, but do the best work of their lives."

—**DR. SUSIE BRUBAKER-COLE,** former Vice Provost for Student Affairs, Stanford University

"The Alchemy of Talent stands at the intersection of data-driven rigor and transformative employee experiences. It is not just a collection of ideas, but a blueprint for pragmatic, data-informed action that can reshape the landscape of team dynamics. This is a win for teams and organizations everywhere."

—**CRAIG A. FUNT,** Senior Vice President, People Strategy and Operations, Qualcomm

"Uncertainty is the norm in today's global competitive environment and necessitates adaptable and resilient teams that embrace critical questioning and integrative thinking. The Alchemy of Talent *offers a practical, science-based guide to building and sustaining teams able to successfully navigate uncertainty and outperform consistently."*

—**SONNY GARG,** former Chief Innovation and Information Officer, Exelon

"Every organization seeks to optimize employee experience while navigating conflicts and uncertainties—fostering an inclusive workplace environment is a crucial step in creating meaningful, sustainable strategies. Dr. Vijay Pendakur is a phenomenal and transformative expert in driving complex organizational change, and his new book is a much-needed primer for every leader committed to maximizing team engagement through evidence-based practices."

—**ARTHUR CHAN,** Vice President of Diversity, Equity, and Inclusion, Planned Parenthood Mar Monte

"As a talent development leader, I'm always looking for that one book that can help every manager drive high performance in their teams. The Alchemy of Talent *blends science and research with practical skills, making it the perfect choice for leading teams through endless uncertainty and disruption that characterizes the world of technology."*

—**DEEPSHIKHA (DEEP) MAHAJAN,** Vice President, Talent Management, Juniper Networks

"As an engineering leader, navigating endless disruption is my norm. But my teams need to be able to do their best work amidst this enduring volatility. The Alchemy of Talent offers team leaders curated behavioral science approaches that are rigorously researched but easy to implement. On top of all that, the book is fun to read, with stories from Dr. Pendakur's years of leading complex teams across multiple industries."

—**ALI ZAFAR**, Vice President of Engineering, Dropbox

"The Alchemy of Talent is a must-read for anyone responsible for designing the employee experience. This science-based blueprint for peak performance is purpose-built for the world of work today: volatile, uncertain, and constantly changing. Team leaders can put the tactics in this book to use immediately and their teams will be more successful for it."

—**SHARON CHOE**, Vice President,
Internal Talent, General Catalyst

"Vijay is a strategic thinker who has presented a clear and compelling approach to managing through challenging times. With disruption now normative in many industries, this is a blueprint that will benefit any team leader."

—**DR. RYAN LOMBARDI**, Vice President for
Student and Campus Life, Cornell University

www.amplifypublishinggroup.com

The Alchemy of Talent: Leading Teams to Peak Performance

Second printing. This Amplify Publishing edition printed in 2024.

For more information, please contact:
Amplify Publishing, an imprint of Amplify Publishing Group
620 Herndon Parkway, Suite 220
Herndon, VA 20170
info@amplifypublishing.com

Library of Congress Control Number: 2024912130

CPSIA Code: PRV1024B

ISBN-13: 979-8-89138-300-5

Printed in the United States

To Marty, 1977-2023.

For the gift of belonging and connection.
Miss you dearly, brother.

The
ALCHEMY
of
TALENT

LEADING TEAMS
TO PEAK
PERFORMANCE

VIJAY PENDAKUR

an imprint of Amplify Publishing Group

CONTENTS

Preface: Are We Done Yet?! xiii

Introduction 1

1   The Case for Complexity 9

2   Catalyst: Psychological Safety 29

3   Catalyst: Belonging 55

4   Catalyst: Connection 79

Conclusion: The Alchemy of You 109

Notes 119

Acknowledgments 127

About the Author 129

PREFACE

Are We Done Yet?!

Disruption Fatigue Is Real

I am drafting the preface to this book in March 2024. Exactly four years ago, my family and I were trying to figure out how to work and live together in an entirely new way due to the COVID-19 pandemic. Before March 2020, I had never had a home office as I tried to manage healthy work/home boundaries by doing all my work *at the office*. We also had a two-year-old and a four-year-old, so my home life was very much focused on managing the rhythms of feeding, changing diapers, cleaning up, and sleeping schedules. My wife, Katie, is a psychotherapist, and her work was deeply tied to being "in the room" with her clients. Our worlds went topsy-turvy in March 2020, and we spent months trying to figure out how to coexist as a sequestered family.

As the spring of 2020 gave way to a long-awaited summer, I found myself trying to understand and adjust to another major disruption: the rise of a complex global activist movement. Suddenly, my news feeds and interpersonal conversations were filled with stories and questions about human dignity, systems of exclusion, and ways to improve societies and organizations to become fairer. It was a lot to take in . . . and I had been working in and around these exact issues for nearly twenty years at that point! But I couldn't remember things ever feeling this expansive, this viscerally painful, or this explosively reactive. I spent months learning and growing and contributing, but I started to feel a growing sense of overwhelm. Between the pandemic and social activism, my brain and my heart needed a beach vacation!

Over the next year, I found a cadence of life that allowed me to do good work, be happy around my family, and look forward to small rewards like family vacations or seeing friends after a long hiatus. As I worked hard to make this "new normal" healthy and sustainable, I began to encounter a word in my news feeds that I hadn't thought of since taking "Intro to Macroeconomics" in college: inflation. At first, like many folks, I just brushed it aside as more clickbait journalism, determined to capture my attention by amping up fear and uncertainty. Unfortunately, this wasn't a hoax, and 2022 brought a whole new disruption into my life: the threat of an economic disaster. Between supply chain shocks, rising prices of consumer goods, and layoffs, I had to learn how to live in *yet another* emerging reality: basic life was palpably more expensive, and the job market felt like quicksand. *Pant...pant...pant...* reality was beginning to feel like sprinting a marathon, and I was not loving it!

Sadly, this cascade of disruption would not be the end of volatility and change in my life. In the spring of 2024, as I draft the preface to this book, nearly every conversation about the world of work features the words "generative artificial intelligence." This was not the case just a year ago. But the emergence of generative AI has cast a fourth boulder into the pond of my life and the ripple effect is just beginning. My brain is aware that disruption and uncertainty are the hallmarks of life in the 21st century, but my spirit feels out of gas. In this state of disconnection, it is easy for me to react poorly to any new change . . . even positive changes.

Am I alone in feeling this way? Nope.

Is this relevant to the world of work? Absolutely.

A Time to Lead Differently

It turns out my story is a lot like the overall story of the workforce. Employees are languishing. Large studies[1] of the global workforce point to low levels of employee engagement. Employees report a sense of "change fatigue" and disconnection in surveys.[2] Many organizations still have not settled into a balance of onsite, remote, and hybrid work that is purpose-built for their business and optimized for team performance.

We also have unique challenges to workforce cohesion resulting from generational diversity.[3] In most industrial societies, there are four active generations in the workplace right now, with baby boomers and gen Z forming the bookends. Each of these generations brings potentially useful differences into the employee experience. But organizations must intentionally engage these differences and upskill leaders to harness them as a strength. Currently, many organizations have been passive in managing this phenomenon, risking team cohesion and overall effectiveness as a result.

Whiplash

Have you ever seen an old black-and-white TV show where a character walks up to a fully set table at a restaurant and whips the tablecloth out from under all the place settings without disturbing anything? I vividly remember seeing this stunt on old TV reruns when I was a kid in the 1980s. I remember asking my parents how the trick worked and, no matter what explanation they offered, I was convinced glue was involved.

The last several years have reminded me of tablecloth whiplash magic. The universe has whipped the tablecloth of workplace context out from under us . . . but this time the trick was not flawlessly executed. As a result, we, the place settings, are scattered. Some of us are upside down. Some of us have found ourselves in a new, unfamiliar place. Some of us aren't even on the table anymore! Some of us are experiencing this disruption with excitement and optimism. Some are struggling with basic questions of meaning and purpose in the new context.

Team and organizational leaders risk disaster if they try to lead like it's "business as usual" now. The employee experience has been disrupted numerous times, and we must lead in ways that are congruent with this shifting context. The leadership norms of the previous decades fall short of what employees now need to unlock their peak potential.

In this vortex of uncertainty and newness, I frequently employ a metaphor to help leaders focus on the real opportunity at hand. Imagine a hiking expedition . . .

The Chasm and the Fog

Imagine you are leading a team of people on a hike through the mountains. As you follow the trail, you suddenly encounter a chasm, a place between two cliffs not connected by a bridge. You must build a bridge across these two cliffs to keep moving forward. Luckily, you have a complex team with you, and they have the diverse perspectives and skills required for this difficult task. You're also in a resource-abundant area, so you have the raw materials necessary for this project. The wind picks up, fog starts rolling in, and visibility gets more difficult.

This is the metaphor for leadership I find myself using most often these days when coaching executives.

Faced with this challenging task (building the bridge) and shifting conditions (fog rolling in), leaders often default to task management: they manage the materials, the key responsibilities, the timelines, and the metrics. I understand the instinct to "get stuff done." Under the immense pressure of executing complex tasks in changing conditions, it is natural to fixate on tangible, tactical managerial commitments.

Imagine that you, as the taskmaster and pacesetter, somehow build the bridge. You let out a sigh of relief and begin to cross the bridge. Halfway across the chasm, you notice a distinct lack of footfalls behind you. You look back. Your team isn't following you.

> *You've completed the task, but you haven't inspired followership.*

This is the conundrum facing leaders in the 21st century. The brilliant manager of the 20th century has all the execution skills to get the bridge built. Our times now call for a different kind of leader, one who can balance the competence of task execution with the skill of cultivating followership.*

---

* Thank you to Molly Anderson and the team at Exponential Talent for introducing me to this beautiful metaphor for leadership.

What's Keeping You Up at Night?

As a speaker and coach, I am regularly engaged with heads of HR for complex organizations. When I ask these leaders one of my favorite discovery questions, "What's keeping you up at night?" here's what I hear:

- We shrunk our organization and now we're growing again. How do we rebuild trust with our employees?
- We have a blend of onsite, remote, and hybrid work styles in our organization. What should our team leaders do to help our teams out-perform now?
- Our employees are tired of change and are resistant to many necessary new organizational efforts. How can we restore resilience and adaptability to our teams?
- Diversity and inclusion are table stakes for us, but these terms have become a lightning rod. How can we continue this work without getting zapped?

While these are tough questions that defy easy answers, I feel better when I hear leaders share these questions with me. Every one of these midnight ruminations demonstrates that strong organizations view talent as one of their greatest assets. To paraphrase Graham Duncan: talent is the best asset class. If organizations recognize this, we can roll up our sleeves and figure out answers to these timely challenges.

Here's the good news: certain factors in employee experience make an outsized difference in individual, team, and organizational performance. What is even more useful, we know which of these factors are particularly well-suited to the conditions described in this preface: volatility, uncertainty, and fatigue. Furthermore, there are models of change that help us move from awareness to skills, and these simple models can help us lead differently, and quickly. All of this adds up to a powerful formula that enables your teams to do the best work of their lives. I call this approach the Alchemy of Talent, and that's what this book is about.

If the last five years had been easy, I probably wouldn't have written this book. From leading at the largest Ivy League university during the first total campus closure in 150 years to leading two different companies through acquisition, volatility and uncertainty seemed to follow my career closely. While these headwinds were often frustrating, they also were productive. They forced me to think differently about how to make the case for unlocking peak performance. In stable times or times of plenty, organizations can be more inclined to invest in their people on faith without much data or evidence. In lean times, and in times of unrest, a leader must be far shrewder.

As a result, I was forced to build models and approaches that made sense to the business. Investments in employees and teams had to be rooted in science and easily measurable. The Alchemy of Talent is the result of my fierce conviction that environments matter and that team leaders have one of the most important roles to play in team members doing the best work of their lives. The model for peak performance you will learn across the following chapters was battle-tested by the numerous friction points of the last several years. Whether you lead a single team or serve as an architect for your organization's people experience, this book will help you build a bridge through the fog and encourage your employees to follow you to success.

The Elephant in the Room

But wait . . . there's an elephant in the room. Vijay has had a LOT of jobs with diversity, equity, and inclusion (DEI) as the focus . . . Is this a DEI book?

As a lifelong student at heart, let me leave you with a multiple-choice answer to this pertinent question (hint hint . . . it's E):

Is This a DEI Book?

A   No. This is a book about how leaders can help their teams do the best work of their lives.

B   Yes. Using the Case for Complexity, you can make a scientific argument for diversity on your team.

C   Yes. If you apply the Alchemy of Talent, your people will feel more included.

D   Maybe. This book invites you to think about DEI differently: as a catalyst for everyone's optimal performance at work.

E   All of the above.

INTRODUCTION

EX = EMPLOYEE EXPERIENCE

Working on HR teams for corporations is actually the second chapter of my career. My first chapter was in higher education. I spent eighteen years working at five different universities in nearly every time zone in the United States. When I share that I worked at universities, most folks assume that I was a faculty member. While that was a route I could have pursued, I chose instead to go after a position that focused on the question that fascinated me most: the relationship between student performance outcomes and the environment in which students experienced their education. I worked in student life, structuring the outside-of-class experience for students so they had a better chance of thriving on campus.

It's a fundamentally accepted truth in education that the environment matters and has a huge effect on students' academic outcomes. If a student is struggling outside of the classroom, due to policies or systems created by the school or campus, you've got a problem. Some of us have experienced this on a personal level. As a speaker, I travel around the country and frequently meet highly successful professionals who struggled in school because of something in the learning environment, not their core cognitive ability. The truism that "environments and experience matter" is table stakes from preschool through undergraduate education. And, somehow, between schooling and the world of work, this fundamental understanding seems to whither and even disappear. While many employers now purport to care about employee experience, well-being, learning, and inclusion, the evidence is often in the budgets. Some of the biggest companies with thousands of employees may only have a skeleton crew driving these employee experience (EX) investments.[1]

My orientation toward the employee experience came from my nearly two decades of working on the student experience when I began the second chapter of my career as a corporate leader. As a university leader, I knew the student was always a key stakeholder, and I was used to finding educational data and evidence to create a case for change on behalf of students. In corporations, I was tasked with leading parts of the talent, culture, and experience investment for employees.

I wasn't as familiar with the workforce research and empirical evidence to support my convictions, but I fundamentally knew that humans needed to be properly supported to thrive. That truism doesn't simply vanish when you swap the student ID for the employee ID.

As I sought to make a case for investing in our people through skills-based training, I unconsciously operated like an academic and went to the research and evidence to justify my roadmap. And boy was I happy. There were endless business cases demonstrating that how employees feel at work, how they feel on a team, and how they feel about their leadership influence, productivity, and results.

I gathered this evidence and started to build a roadmap to improve the employee experience. But, as the macroeconomy began to tighten in 2021 and beyond, I began to hear more requests from the board or the executives to "have it make sense for the business." This friction was helpful. It forced discipline and rigor in how I made the case for EX investments that would ultimately show up as operating expenses on our balance sheets.

This book is the culmination of a multi-year process of making EX "work for the business." Numerous headwinds forced me to consistently make a business case for investing in EX that a CFO or COO would support. The cases that won most frequently were individual, team, and organizational performance outcomes. I began to craft a logic model that showed how specific, measurable factors in EX connected and laddered up to deliver real ROI to the organization.

As a consultant and speaker, I also engage with hundreds of people and leaders across the globe. I often ask these leaders, "What employee experience factors are critical to your teams doing the best work of their lives?" And even senior HR executives give me mixed, fuzzy answers. This happened so often that I began to suspect that most organizations could benefit from having a clear, simple model for investing in their people and teams. Do this, not that. The Alchemy of Talent is my formula to help organizations win more consistently through a clear, simple EX blueprint: complexity, psychological safety, belonging, and connection.

How to Use This Book

An optimized EX ecosystem creates wins for the individual, the team, and the organization. That's the bumper sticker that every organizational and team leader should have on their car. It's not pithy, but it is accurate. This book is an articulation of how we can position concepts, research, data, and behavior to unlock wins at all three levels. I call this the Threefold Win: wins for the individual, the team, and the organization. Organizing an EX model and strategy from the Threefold Win shifts the value proposition from feel-good vibes to ROI: individuals will excel at work, teams will outperform, and the organization will flourish.

Each chapter is also organized around a core concept to enhance the EX ecosystem. Each concept comes from years of studying research and data and has been selected for its applicability and utility in the world of work. While there are myriad concepts one could focus on, these create a flywheel for your organization in ways that merit keen investment and measurement.

In working with organizational leaders and intact teams over the years, I've created a radically simplified model for behavioral change called "Knowing It, Spotting It, Doing It" that leads to stronger, more measurable individual and team outcomes. After the Case for Complexity, each chapter will follow this same model. Here I will first introduce you to each key concept:

Knowing It: In this section you will encounter the concept in a way that helps you make sense of it in your personal life and as a leader of an organization or team. This section will also showcase relevant research that substantiates the concept as a key driver of performance and success.

Spotting It: You'll then be engaged in a section that challenges you to identify how this concept

The Alchemy of Talent

Individual
Personal Growth
Job Satisfaction
Career Advancement

Team
Improved Collaboration
Peak Performance
Enhanced Resilience

Threefold Win

Organization
Retain Top Talent
Increased Profitability
Optimal Employer Brand

shows up in individuals, teams, and organizations. Identifying what behaviors either enhance or diminish the concept, as well as what it looks like when a culture embodies the concept, is a key leadership sense-making skill that can help leaders move beyond the behavioral science approach into the organizational design and development tasks that make this flywheel spin.

Doing It: Finally, each chapter will offer you an example of a behavioral investment you can make to drive a Threefold Win by weaving it into individual, team, and organizational behavior. This section will help you make a change by focusing on actual workplace skills that turn up the volume on the beneficial parts of your EX ecosystem.

In addition to introducing leaders to new concepts and approaches, this book sharpens leaders' thinking by offering several diagnostic tools to take what they've learned in each chapter and begin the process of applying this learning to their own teams or organizations. Each chapter is sprinkled with a list of questions for you to consider. These questions are helpful in scanning your current EX ecosystem and considering what changes are necessary to unlock peak performance for your people.

Before I close this introduction, I want to invite you to think about the phrase "productive friction." Think about a time that your ideas or way of doing things have been challenged, in a healthy way, by a friend or colleague. This challenge then resulted in you *improving as a result of friction*. Every high-performing leader I've spoken to has plenty of these moments in their life . . . but what's really going on here? It's not random. It's not magic. It's science.

1

The Case for Complexity

In an earlier stage of my career, I vividly remember launching a national job search as my first step into a senior leadership role. I'd had a phenomenal five-year experience as a director in a dynamic university setting and had used this platform to build a national reputation within higher education. I presented my work at conferences, consulted on the side, and took on a number of high-visibility stretch projects to prepare for my next step into being an associate vice president (AVP). I talked to my peers and friends and built a search plan. It was go time!

Or so I thought.

A year into the official job search, I'd applied for well over a dozen AVP roles I was fully qualified for and in geographic markets where my family was willing to move.

Crickets. I never even got a phone interview.

Something was deeply wrong. I was embarrassed and ashamed. I remember mustering up the courage to tell my friend Ann Marie about how I was getting nowhere. She listened compassionately and said, "Let me introduce you to Jill. She can help." I remember looking Jill up online and thinking, "Hmm, this person has nothing in common with me . . . Is this going to be helpful?" Still, I really wanted to advance my career, so I reached out to Jill, and we set up a time to chat.

Splash!

The conversation with Jill was a bucket of ice water to the face. Her perspective was completely foreign to me, and I felt really uncomfortable during the entire phone call. She shared numerous examples of how people navigated the climb from mid-level to senior level, and she had plenty of specific strategies and tactics for me to consider. At one point in the conversation she asked me, "Who are you seeking advice from in this job search?" I shared a list of names with her. She spent a few minutes asking for more details and then she gently pointed out, "Everyone on your board of directors is like you . . . They have mid-level jobs with similar backgrounds. *How are they supposed to advise you on getting roles that they don't hold themselves?*"

It was a true "lightbulb" moment and a gift that I am still grateful for today.

In the months that followed that conversation, I changed my process dramatically, and I saw different results. I ended up with a phenomenal job offer that truly served as an inflection point in my career trajectory. And it wouldn't have happened without friction.

When I look back on that magical call with Jill, our differences served me well. Jill is in a different generation than me. She has held many senior roles. She is a White woman who worked in higher education before going into the for-profit, corporate world. Her complex perspective was rooted in her life experience, which was very different than mine. My ideas about job searching became *better* due to the productive friction between us.

🧪 **CHALLENGE YOURSELF**

Identify a time that friction has resulted in your improvement. This could be a moment where your ideas improved, your body became stronger, or your emotional intelligence evolved due to shock, agitation, challenge, or stress.

Consider the case of my friend and colleague Sonny Garg. Sonny often tells a story about a moment of profound friction in his life. After a meteoric first chapter of his career involving a high-profile role at the White House, Sonny ended up at Exelon, a Fortune 125 company. He worked hard, was brilliant, and rose to a C-level role in the organization. His ambition and drive had allowed him to "check a lot of boxes" in his journey. He had material success, a family, and lots of public significance. One day, he was having lunch with a good friend of his, Tim. Sonny describes Tim as a "contrast" to himself. Both people are highly successful, but Tim is very different from Sonny in meaningful ways. Sonny was telling Tim about being appointed to the executive committee at Exelon, and in the middle of his storytelling, Sonny ended up saying, "Tim, my life sucks." The admission came from somewhere deep and somewhere surprising for Sonny. Tim replied with six words that changed Sonny's life: "What are you chasing, and why?"

Sonny went home that night and used Tim's question to look at every part of his life, personal and professional. The friction of Tim's perspective and question caused a cascade in Sonny's life that led to Sonny making profound changes in his worldview and life choices. Sonny didn't have a good answer to Tim's question, but a heartfelt pursuit of answers led Sonny to a new chapter of his life that felt more integrated, purposeful, and healthy to Sonny. Without friction, Sonny wouldn't have a transformational inflection point.

Now let's flip the script and talk about you. Take a minute to think about advice contrary to your viewpoint that resulted in a better outcome for you. Think about when you've experienced discomfort when met with new perspectives. Friction is rarely fun! Successful people have to change their approaches constantly to adapt to volatility and ambiguity in their personal and professional lives. Having mentors and advisors who offer you the gift of friction can make all the difference.

One way to understand improvement through friction—or shock—is through the concept of antifragility, coined by the economist Nassim Taleb.[1] Antifragility is a key idea for this book, so let's walk through it carefully. Taleb explains that *"some things benefit from shocks; they thrive and grow when exposed to volatility, randomness, disorder, and stressors and love adventure, risk, and uncertainty."* Taleb coined the term because he found that, in the world of economics, there were only two concepts: things that were fragile and broke under shock, and things that were robust, that withstood shock. But, what about things that actually improve from shock?

Returning to my career search, my ideas and process on career navigation became considerably better in response to friction, or the shock, introduced by Jill's experience and perspective. For my job search process to be an antifragile process, it took more than simple friction. For me to experience the benefits of friction, I had to be willing to change my thinking, and I had to invite challenge, disruption, discomfort, and humility into my approach. In my story of job searching, antifragility—or the phenomenon of improvement in response to shock—became possible because of the presence of friction *and* my response to it.

So, what does that have to do with the Alchemy of Talent? How do we get from the concepts of friction and the readiness to harness its power to the Threefold Win? To understand the potential gains of unlocking antifragility in EX, we have to first map out the current landscape of organizational diversity.

"Houston, we have noise . . ."

In my work with engineers, I've seen firsthand the quest for better signal-to-noise ratios. In non-engineering terms, signal is the thing we want, and noise is everything else. In human systems, like EX ecosystems, everywhere we apply intentionality, budgets, processes, or effort to make a difference in the EX offers us a chance to consider signal and noise. And, as dynamic system pros can attest to, attaining a "clean signal" is really challenging. People are messy, the world is chaotic, and our best efforts are often loaded with noise.

The signal and noise framework is a useful mental model when thinking about "diversity." The word appears to trigger a wide variety of emotions from its equally wide array of definitions. This means, in the diversity space, we have *really* bad signal-to-noise ratios, and in our current moment of political polarization, it appears to be getting worse. This may be a moment of complete "signal disruption," like when your phone simply can't get a connection at all! Hello? Hello? Am I in a dead spot?

When speaking and consulting, I often ask leaders, "Why is diversity important for your team?" It's a simple question that can catch really smart leaders flat-footed. After a few *umms* and *ahhs*, I hear a variety of answers, most of which are loaded with noise.

A clear articulation of the value proposition of diversity is critical if we are going to sustain it across our people ecosystems. If you're like most leaders, you've likely heard one or more of these propositions, so let's dive into them in greater depth.

1. The "Diversity Helps Us Sell More" Value Proposition

This value proposition comes up frequently in business-to-consumer (B2C) companies. The clean signal here is: "Diversity in our company makes us relevant to our diverse customers, and helps us build products and experiences that serve these audiences more effectively." The noise in this signal is: "Diversity is simply a tactic for companies to make more money." While this emphasizes the profitability ROI of diversity, it also places the spotlight on employees from diverse groups to potentially just sell to "their own community." For example, in a consumer products brand that is trying to expand its base of women customers, the women hired onto the team may be seen as a gimmicky investment in helping only "sell to women."

2. The "Repairing Harm" Value Proposition

This proposition comes from the realization that some groups of people have been structurally barred from full participation in society through a variety of systemic and interpersonal practices of exclusion. As a result, most organizations believe they should invest in diversity to repair this harm. The clean signal on this value proposition is: "Diversity is the right thing to do for our society, and it will benefit historically underserved and excluded groups." The noise associated with this signal is: "Diversity efforts only benefit oppressed groups." This can elicit defensive postures in groups who begin to ask, "What am I losing in order for others to gain?"

3. The "Diversify Leadership" Value Proposition

This proposition is rooted in the desire to link an organization's profitability or success to its leadership diversity. Around 2013, some business leaders argued that highly successful companies tended to have more diverse executive leadership and board representation. Efforts were made to ground this claim by studying large companies, and evidence emerged that supported this value proposition. The clean signal here is: "If diversifying our executive layer and our boards leads to increased profitability, then this is something we all want, right?" This signal gained more momentum in 2013 when Sheryl Sandberg's "Lean In" efforts began championing gender diversity on boards, and when McKinsey committed to a biennial release of their 2015 report[2] on how diversity and profitability are linked in certain companies.

Unfortunately, this signal is loaded with noise. First, diversity is often defined as race and gender, due to how widely available this data is in the United States. Since these categories of data are more consistently available, researchers use this data to make the argument. However, an unintended consequence of years of reporting on "diversity gains" by showcasing only two categories of diversity has conflated the very definition of diversity with just race and gender. Second, the evidence of profitability often triggers skepticism from business leaders who see this as correlative rather than causative data. To put it plainly, when I share this value proposition with senior business executives, they often respond with, "Well, those companies were already highly successful, and they used their vast resources to go out and buy the diversity later." Last, this signal has the noise of emphasizing diversity just in the top levels of organizations, which feeds into the performative tactic of hiring a few executives who look different, so the company can achieve the optics of caring about diversity.

The turbulent diversity landscape I describe in the preface of this book shows why signal and noise challenges are particularly troubling right now. In times of polarization, it's even more important to have a value proposition for diversity that is well-calibrated to the context. In pointing out the noise challenges with the diversity value propositions above, I am not saying that these are illegitimate or unhelpful. Rather, the adage by statistician George Box applies here: "All models are flawed, some are useful."

These value propositions may lead to confusion or misunderstanding generally about the case for diversity, and they also increase the risk of reputational harm in the current landscape by playing right into the politicized attacks on diversity.

A Better Way . . .

What if we could frame a value proposition for diversity that both emphasized the return on investment for the organization *and* benefitted every individual and team in the organization? Luckily, there's a way to position diversity as a Threefold Win if we tap into the science of antifragility and friction.

Diversity can be understood as a mix of inherent and acquired traits, according to organizational psychologists.[3,4] Inherent traits include where you were born, your native language, whether you are right-hand or left-hand dominant, or your economic status in early childhood. You don't control these things, but they have a powerful shaping influence over how you understand yourself, others, and the world around you.

Acquired traits are things like second languages, your caregiver status for elders or children, or your current economic class status. These are factors that are more fungible throughout your life but still serve as invisible lenses to understand yourself, others, and the world around you.

🧪 CHALLENGE YOURSELF

Take a minute to consider your inherent and acquired traits. How do these shape the point of view you bring to work?

When we expand our definition of diversity from narrow, legally protected categories like race and gender to a more comprehensive understanding of inherent and acquired traits, we unlock the power of a new, clean signal: every person is a latticework of complexity through their inherent and acquired traits. This complexity has considerable bearing on how each of us understands ourselves, engages with others, and sees the world.

A clean signal allows us to frame the value proposition of diversity to enhance complexity. If we pursue a truly diverse mix of employees in our organizations and on our teams, we will bake in complexity to our people ecosystems. But why is complexity actually helpful?

Complexity serves as friction, so let's double back to the concept of antifragility now to see how it all ties together to unleash the Alchemy of Talent.

Antifragile things don't just survive shock; they improve because of jostling, rubbing, and challenging. When we look at high-performance individuals, teams, and organizations, the science holds true. Most organizations exist to create value through developing products, processes, ideas, people, or solutions. When people work on collaborative teams to drive an organization's outcomes, these teams are expected to produce innovative solutions to complex problems. More homogenous teams have less friction to help them innovate. These teams could be considered "sites of sameness," and they are at risk of generating fragile outcomes by unwittingly falling prey to groupthink. The products, ideas, or services they create are missing the productive force of friction from the design/test process, and this could produce something that breaks under shock.

Back in 2017, Pepsi attempted to capture the zeitgeist of social protest, Black Lives Matter, and police brutality. But they clearly lacked productive friction on their marketing team because they released an ad that alienated millions of viewers and cost them financially. The now infamous "Kendall Jenner ad" features an abstract depiction of a protest and of the police managing the protest. Kendall Jenner is in the middle of a modeling shoot and appears to notice the protest, causing her to leave the shoot and attend the event. She weaves through the crowd, grabs a Pepsi, and offers it to a police officer. The moment where the cop accepts the can of soda is captured by a photographer who appears to be a hijab-wearing Muslim woman. The photographer smiles as she takes the photo, implying warmth, acceptance, and progress. The ad is loaded with various social symbols and appears to communicate that Pepsi itself may be a cure to complex issues between underserved communities and the police.

The gap between public sentiment and the messages in the Pepsi ad was indescribably large and people were offended by Pepsi's choices. While I do not know the exact composition of the marketing team that put this ad concept together, the final product speaks to a lack of friction. If anyone in the creative team had been involved in a protest, they might have raised the point that this ad is a caricature of social movements rather than an authentic representation of what's happening on the ground. Or, if someone on the team identified as Muslim, they may have asked, "Why is the photographer smiling and wearing a hijab? What are we trying to communicate with this choice?" Finally, productive friction from differences could have saved Pepsi from the self-inflicted wound of implying that a can of soda can build a bridge between underserved communities and the police.

In contrast, complex teams, loaded with inherent and acquired diverse traits, have built-in friction that contributes to antifragile outcomes. The diversity of these teams can be an advantage. It offers the team plenty of opportunities to question assumptions, think differently, and capitalize on outlier viewpoints.

Scientists examined this phenomenon in an experimental study conducted across two continents using teams of financially literate participants.[5] These participants were given extensive financial data on made-up companies. The task across the two experiment sites was the same: to identify the stock price of these companies based on the data provided. The controlled variable in the experiment was the composition of the teams. Some teams were intentionally constructed to be very homogenous across multiple factors such as age, race, gender, and more. Other teams were constructed to be more diverse using this same composite index of diversity. **The diverse teams were 58 percent more likely to pick the stock price of the companies accurately**. While this is a significant finding, the explanation provided by the researchers is even more important.

In observing the teams' processes during the experiment, these scientists concluded that the diverse teams had built-in friction that "upended conformity and enhanced deliberation . . ."

This friction was the difference-maker in the study, and it ties back to the science of antifragility.

Complexity unlocks productive friction. When searching for a career opportunity, I got nowhere in my job search because I sought advice from people who were like me. Jill was different than me in several meaningful ways: age, seniority, generational perspective, gender, race, and industry alignment. These differences upended conformity with the advice I'd previously received and enhanced my deliberation when Jill and I analyzed why I couldn't get the AVP job.

For organizational leaders seeking to optimize performance with their people and teams, complexity is a key ingredient. When we assemble complex teams, we harness the power of antifragile ideation in service of our organization's goals and competitive outcomes. Broadly pursuing diversity, beyond just race and gender, is a powerful way to fast-track inherent and acquired differences into your teams, which can set the foundation for a Threefold Win. Furthermore, complexity increases *relevance*. The world is a complex place, and sameness inside your organization creates the risk of irrelevance . . . You may miss out on what your customers or stakeholders need from you due to your homogeneity.

In this time of social polarization, the commonly used value propositions of diversity are too loaded with noise to provide optimal service to organizational and team leaders. The Case for Complexity offers EX champions a low-noise way to a) frame the pursuit of diversity in their people ecosystem that is tied to the science of antifragility, b) avoid the landmines in the current socio-political landscape, and c) cleanly link the investment in diversity to individual, team, and organization-level *performance outcomes*. This is a value proposition that allows EX leaders to build momentum and attract a wide base of allies.

 CHALLENGE YOURSELF

What is the current value proposition for diversity in your team or organization? Is this well under-stood and socialized across the leadership? Is this value proposition serving your team/organization well right now? Are you able to consist-ently tie it to outcomes that position diversity as a win for the individual, team, and organization?

Okay, so you've got complex teams in your organization. Congrats! You're ready for the Alchemy of Talent. Oh wait, here's the catch: friction requires a *few* cata-lysts to activate the magic of antifragility. Just like in my story of searching for an AVP job, friction alone didn't create improvement in my process; I had to add my own humility, agility, and emotional intelligence to the mix. I also had to feel respected by Jill, even as I was being challenged in numerous ways.

Forcing friction in your people's ecosystem without any guardrails can look quite uninviting, painful, or even abusive. This goes back to the reality that simply assembling highly diverse groups of people and saying, "Have at it!" has rarely ended well, because people need a behavioral toolbox that allows them to harness the power of this complexity. Without the toolbox, we get a workplace filled with daily "oops" and "ouch" moments that result in lower productivity, less innovation, and higher attrition. Let's open this toolbox and see what we can do to turn friction into antifragility for our complex teams! In each of the following three chapters, you will encounter one of these powerful catalysts in the Alchemy of Talent.

2

Catalyst: Psychological Safety

A few years ago, scientists conducted an observational study of sixty-two pharmaceutical teams racing to develop products in an extremely competitive marketplace.[1] These teams worked in high-pressure environments, navigating complex regulatory requirements and meeting tight deadlines, all while bringing new drugs to market. The researchers created a multi-factor index of diversity (i.e., more than race and gender) to map team complexity and collected objective team performance data from senior company leaders. Knowing what you now know about complexity, friction, and antifragility, would you guess that the most diverse teams performed the best?

I know I sure did.

But the team performance data tells a more nuanced story. Some of the diverse teams performed far better than average, but some of the diverse teams performed worse than average. Why wasn't the built-in friction of diversity consistently driving peak performance?

Luckily, the researchers collected information on another factor that could help explain this distribution of performance outcomes: psychological safety.

Every study participant completed surveys assessing the psychological safety of their team environment. The highly diverse teams with low psychological safety largely underperformed, even when compared to more homogenous teams. The diverse teams with the highest psychological safety achieved some of the highest performance outcomes of any teams in the study.

So, what's the solution?

As I shared before, we need catalysts to unlock the Alchemy of Talent. Complexity alone won't get us there, but psychological safety is the perfect place to start. Let's see how we can turn up the volume on this incredible catalyst.

Knowing It

Have you ever been afraid to share something with a manager because you were anxious about being shamed or punished? It's a terrible feeling and something most of us can relate to. It also speaks right to the heart of psychological safety.

Psychological Safety: One's willingness to take risks, admit failure, or challenge authority without fear of shame or punishment.[2]

In all my years of speaking at companies and coaching executives, no one has ever encountered this definition of psychological safety and said, "Nah, I'm not interested in that for myself or my team!" The most powerful behavioral science tools we have elicit wide appreciation because we can feel their value on a personal level. Everyone knows what it is like to stick their neck out (proverbially) when they feel safe and encouraged. They also know how painful it can be when they don't feel safe. Yet, our near-universal desire for psychological safety does not mean we know how to create and sustain this powerful catalyst at work. This innate desire is one of the reasons organizational psychologists began writing about non-physical safety in the 1960s,[3] and the concept really picked up momentum when Amy Edmondson began focusing her research on it in the 1990s.[4]

In popular discussions of psychological safety, people often gravitate toward the ultimate expression of this catalyst: a team member challenging their manager. In my years of work with complex teams, I've noticed that speaking up to a manager is dependent on several other supports. Challenging a leader is an extreme form of risk-taking, and, while we often say we want to be challenged as leaders, we need to understand this heroic act as only being possible if several other supports, or scaffolds, are in place for your team members.

Timothy Clark's "4 Stages of Psychological Safety" model[5] is a productive way to describe the scaffolding of psychological safety, so I'll touch on it here. Clark asks us

The Heroic Act Without the Scaffolds

to think about the heroic moment where a team member challenges a leader as the final stage for psychological safety. For individuals to incur this kind of risk consistently on a team or across an organization, he argues that humans first need:

- **Inclusion Safety:** to feel valued and seen for who you are.
- **Learner Safety:** to be encouraged and supported to make mistakes as a part of learning.

- **Contributor Safety:** to be given the autonomy and guidance to make meaningful contributions.

And when these three scaffolds are present, we increase the chances of consistent "Challenger Safety," or heroic moments where team members productively challenge leaders, resulting in better outcomes for teams and organizations.

CATALYST: PSYCHOLOGICAL SAFETY **33**

Psychological Safety as a Catalyst for Performance

Early in my career, I was an assistant director in a department. When my manager left suddenly for a new role, I was asked to cover the vacant director role as an interim director, and I met with the AVP who would manage me in this interim appointment. I can vividly remember one of our first real meetings. He'd prepared a few questions for me and one of them was, "What do you think the reputation of your department is across the division?" I answered earnestly . . . and I completely missed the mark. Not only did I miss a chance to demonstrate leadership acumen to my new boss, but I also revealed that I was woefully unaware of the broader organizational environment I'd been working in. Until that point, I'd largely kept my head down and focused on my relatively small scope of work.

Looking back, my new boss could easily have dismissed me, citing that I didn't have innate leadership potential at that point. But I received the oddest assignment at the end of that meeting. He asked me to go meet with half a dozen directors of influential units across the organization and get their perspectives on my department. It was a complete wake-up call for me. Actually, it was two wake-up calls: first, I realized my department had a weak reputation, which was shocking to me; second, and more importantly, I realized how uninformed I was because I was isolated. The second realization caused a ripple effect in my approach to work that shapes my leadership to this day: always gather an external stakeholder perspective.

I met with my manager again a few weeks later and shared what I'd learned in my discovery tour. I felt energized to fix some of the problems that I was now aware of. My manager was calm, supportive, and probably smiling inside! I ended up getting the directorship role, and I worked for that manager for six more years. Those were some of the most high-performance years of my career, primarily because I had all four components of psychological safety while working under that manager: 1) I felt valued for who I was, 2) I was given the space to learn by making mistakes, 3) I was allowed to contribute in numerous ways, and 4) I challenged his thinking and leadership in key moments.

CHALLENGE YOURSELF

Think back on high-performance seasons of your career, when you felt able to challenge a leader. Identify how you felt scaffolded toward Challenger Safety by considering the three preceding stages of psychological safety in the Clark model.

Famously, and tragically, psychological safety was a factor in the 1986 Challenger shuttle disaster. In the after-action analysis, NASA determined that the shuttle exploded due to a failure in the O-rings. Further investigation revealed that numerous NASA employees had attempted to raise concerns about these O-rings but had been shut down or ignored. Others witnessed this and remained silent with their concerns. In op-ed pieces after the tragedy, insiders shared that NASA had a culture that ignored critical feedback and a bureaucracy that made it very difficult to blow the whistle on mission critical concerns. Cultures that position critique as a "barrier to speed" or even insubordination are cultures of low psychological safety and they create tremendous risk.

Psychological safety is a performance catalyst in my life and probably in yours, but it's not just isolated to personal anecdotes or news stories. It also shows up in the research on highly successful teams and organizations. Looking back, it shows up as a difference-maker in the drug development study at the start of this chapter. Psychological safety correlated with the highest-performing diverse teams.

It's also seen in the now famous example from Google's research on high-performing teams. Beginning in 2012, Google launched Project Aristotle, a study of 180 internal teams.[6] This monumental effort involved gathering employee sentiment by conducting over fifty thousand pulse surveys over the course of a multi-year study. Scientists consistently monitored the performance outcomes of these teams and developed a performance-ranking scale. As a result, the organizational researchers in Project Aristotle found five key factors that consistently showed up for the highest-performing teams. And out of these five factors, psychological safety was the most significant. The teams with the highest psychological safety consistently ranked the highest in performance.

The Alchemy of Talent: The Value of Psychological Safety for Complex Teams

Psychological safety, as a leading source of organizational health, is paramount. But how do you generate and sustain it? As you'll recall, teams need complex friction to unlock antifragility and achieve better outcomes. We need shock. It's necessary for the development of ideas, processes, and products to improve because of disruption. So, if we want a self-reliant state of antifragility, we need to understand how people experience friction and differences in the workplace.

It can feel painful when you are challenged with feedback or your ideas have holes poked in them. We can question whether we are valued or respected on the team if the conditions are not primed for healthy, productive friction. Similarly, when you are working on a team, facing deadlines and other pressures, key differences across the team can feel like barriers to easy collaboration. Investing in all four stages of psychological safety is a necessary catalyst in taking the friction that comes from complexity and making it a productive force rather than an engine for demoralization and reduced outcomes.

Once again, we see this play out in the study of drug development teams. The more diverse teams that reported low psychological safety underperformed against the average. The authors of the study write that these teams faced ". . . communication challenges that get in the way of their undeniable potential."[7] Without psychological safety, differences inside the teams became a limiting factor. The researchers also looked at team satisfaction and found another important correlation: the most diverse teams that reported low levels of psychological safety were also the unhappy teams. And, as you may have guessed already, the more diverse teams with high levels of psychological safety reported better than average levels of satisfaction. In essence, psychological safety helps make complexity a driver for people enjoying their work experience.

Without the catalyst of psychological safety, EX leaders cannot begin to unlock the Alchemy of Talent, even if they are fortunate enough to have an organization with complex teams.

Spotting It: Scanning Your Environment

In my work across dozens of organizations, I've found it helpful to not just explain what a concept is and why it is important (that's why we start with Knowing It), but to ultimately help leaders visualize what the ideal state looks like for their organization. Behavior is highly contextual, and what psychological safety looks like on a retail team that is customer-facing may be wildly different than how this behavior shows up on a team of researchers in a think tank. Identifying what "good" looks like is an important sense-making skill of EX leaders.

Having a clear vision for how these concepts show up as behaviors is also useful in moving from awareness to action as EX leaders are often charged with developing skill-building experiences for their organization.

Examples of Psychological Safety at Work*		
	Good	**Great**
The Safe Individual	Taking on a challenging stretch assignment to learn new skills.	Giving a manager feedback on how something could be done better.
The Safe Team Leader	During a major organizational change, naming the unknown for the team: "I don't know what's going to happen . . ."	Leader who admits mistakes to the team, takes ownership, and takes actions to improve.

---

* Learning new concepts is cool. Changing your behavior is even better. Visit *The Alchemy of Talent* page on my site (QR code in the back of this book) to download a tool that helps you apply psychological safety at work.

Examples of Psychological Safety at Work*		
	Good	**Great**
The Safe Organization	An organization that has a strong track record of internal mobility. Employees are safe to learn and grow and choose to stay by trying new roles in the organization, rather than leave for a promotion.	An organization regularly benefits from spirited disagreement within teams, resulting in improved decision-making and outcomes.

How psychological safety shows up at work can vary greatly across industries and organizations, as culture and behavior are deeply contextual. The table above is meant to illustrate an exercise you can do with your team or key leaders in your organization.

Doing It: Generating and Sustaining Psychological Safety at Work

In a people ecosystem, team leaders are a key driver of team performance. This is not just because they manage the tasks, expectations, and delivery of the team, but also because they have the power to establish important

---

* Learning new concepts is cool. Changing your behavior is even better. Visit *The Alchemy of Talent* page on my site (QR code in the back of this book) to download a tool that helps you apply psychological safety at work.

behavioral conditions like psychological safety. In this Doing It section, I can't cover every relevant tactic. The good news is that there are countless ways to increase psychological safety on teams. But it's not enough to be able to Know It and Spot It; the Alchemy of Talent requires that we exhibit behaviors and practice skills to make psychological safety happen. Here are two leader commitments that appear frequently in best practice research and that I have used as a coach/facilitator in over a decade of leading my own teams and empowering other team leaders.

 CHALLENGE YOURSELF

Take a minute to think about what "good" looks like for you as an individual. How do you behave when you feel psychologically safe at work?

Technique 1: Inquire and Affirm

There are certain moments that have an outsized effect on the team's willingness to continue to take risks, admit failure, and challenge ideas. How a leader responds to feedback or challenges is one of these moments. Feedback is a powerful signal of trust from the team member, and what a leader signals back can amplify psychological safety, both for the individual delivering the feedback and for team members who witness the moment.

I emphasize the need for leaders to slow down our instinctive twitchy brain, which is always there, always ready to fight, flee, or freeze. Our twitchy brain is evolutionarily hardwired and not that helpful at work! Consider the following scenario:

You've been leading an intact team for over six months when a new trend has emerged in your industry that's really shaking things up. As a result, the economics of your space have changed, and your team is under pressure to adjust its roadmap and move more quickly. You are expected to lead this shift. Your team is stressed out, spread thin, and beginning to worry about the future. You pull the team together to brainstorm a solution to a key problem, and in the middle of this meeting, a team member raises their hand and says, "I feel like we've been here before. I mean, you pulled us together less than a month ago for one of these exercises and now we're here again. This is getting kinda frustrating." Their tone is respectful, but their face and energy signal real frustration.

Immediately, your twitchy brain starts whispering:

"Don't they know how hard I've been working too? I can't help that the goalposts keep changing!"

"I can't believe they're calling me out in front of the whole group! Will the team lose respect for me now?"

"Is there an eject button in this conference room? Can I just catapult this person into space?"

Okay, so that last thought is a bit of a joke but maybe not too far off from how you or I have felt in these tense moments. Our twitchy brains have kicked into a full "fight or flight" response and are giving us a variety of "meanings" to help us understand the moment. How we understand the moment has a huge bearing on how we will choose to act. Unfortunately, these "meanings" are loaded with noise . . . They are potentially inaccurate and harmful, and they are not going to position us to act in ways that bolster psychological safety.

When a leader responds poorly to feedback, it is often in response to not having a technique to slow down their response process, resulting in them acting on impulse. I have compassion for this experience because it is all too human, especially when the leader is just as stressed, tired, and anxious as the team! But leaders generally want their teams to do their best work, so psychological safety is a key asset, especially in these crucible moments.

The behavioral bio-hack I use to work around this scenario is to Inquire and Affirm.

There are numerous models illustrating how to respond to challenges or feedback, and many are useful. As part of my personalized approach, I boiled a lot of these down to Inquire and Affirm. It's super simple, which increases the chance that we remember and use it under stress.

Inquire is a call for curiosity. So, when you are challenged with feedback, use curiosity to slow down your twitchy brain and buy yourself time. To practice this step, I coach leaders to remember the phrase, "Tell me more . . ." as a signal of curiosity. When you find yourself on the receiving end of feedback and you feel your heartbeat

accelerating, your mouth going dry, and your internal monologue going into panic mode, remember to slow down. Respond with curiosity first. "Tell me more . . ." or some other form of curious inquiry buys you time to listen more, breathe, and calm your twitchy brain down. In the space of a deep breath, you can remind yourself that our goal is to sustain a high sense of psychological safety, so how we respond in this moment matters.

The second part of this behavioral model is to Affirm. Affirm does not mean agree. Feedback and challenge come in all forms, and sometimes it isn't even valid. But the act of a team member giving feedback signals trust and you, as the leader, have a responsibility to maintain that trust and amplify psychological safety by affirming their choice to trust you. By slowing down the twitchy brain, we get the chance to use a practiced form of affirmation: to acknowledge that you've heard the person and to thank them for stepping forward and offering feedback. Notice that you're affirming that you hear what they're saying and that they gave you feedback. This doesn't mean you have to publicly or immediately agree with the feedback. If you can see feedback as valid and helpful in the moment, acknowledge this. In truly stressful experiences, it can be hard to sort out how we really feel about a piece of feedback. So, the Affirm step reminds us to clearly signal that you've listened and express support and appreciation for their choice to give you feedback. And then, if you need it, ask for time to consider, and respond to them in a day or two.

Let's return to the scenario from before and see how

Inquire and Affirm can help a leader invest in psychological safety:

Team member: *"I feel like we've been here before. I mean, you pulled us together less than a month ago for one of these exercises and now we're here again. This is getting kinda frustrating."*

Leader: *"Hey, thanks for stepping up. Can you tell me more about how this feels like the same thing we did a month ago?"*

(Breathe. Breathe. Breathe while they share more. Listen to what they are feeling. What is their emotional truth?)

Leader: *"I'm hearing your frustration with how intense and unpredictable the last few weeks have been. Thanks for letting me know that this brainstorming session feels like something we've already done. I appreciate you stepping forward and naming your perspective. Let me consider it for a bit and get back to you on how the team can solve problems going forward. Can we talk tomorrow, one to one?"*

By using the Inquire and Affirm approach in this stressful situation, the leader has increased the chance that the team will continue to have enough trust to speak up in the future. The team member who offered the feedback knows that there is a follow-up action coming tomorrow, and the entire group saw how the leader affirmed the choice to give feedback and offered to consider it carefully. In the one-to-one meeting the next day, this leader may decide to disagree with the team member's assessment and offer a counter-perspective.

Maintaining psychological safety does not mean abdicating your perspective or responsibility as the team leader. But leaders can disagree in ways that still signal, "I don't agree with your feedback, but I see your perspective and appreciate you taking the risk to share it. You are safe with me." This is a leadership skill worth cultivating through consistent practice, as it is a powerful way to generate and maintain psychological safety and peak performance on your team.

Technique 2: Setting Team Norms

In one of my first leadership-level roles, I reported to a vice president who was intent on creating and sustaining a high-performance team in a particularly challenging organizational culture and system. She hired a coach for our leadership team who worked with us in an ongoing process to help us do our best work despite some of the conditions that we could not control.

I remember being excited and a bit nervous about going to my first leadership team gathering with this group. I'd anticipated that we'd start the morning by discussing our strategic plan or looking at the budget for the next year. But, when we got started that morning, the vice president said, "We're going to get started by creating our team's Rules of Engagement." We spent the first part of the morning having an open discussion on how we wanted to communicate, interact, and hold each other accountable as a team. We generated a list of commitments and spent time stack-ranking this list and cutting some items. By the afternoon, we had a Rules of Engagement document that everyone felt invested in. This document did not get shelved as an artifact of that offsite. Every time we gathered in the vice president's conference room, it was up on the wall, reminding us of what we'd committed to. And, at future offsites, we took a smaller amount of time to revisit the Rules of Engagement and consider modifications to the list. It was a living document.

I didn't know it at the time, but this was a best practice example of how to increase and sustain psychological safety for a team. The coach helped us insert principles of feedback into the list of rules, like a commitment to speaking up early and often and a commitment that the feedback recipient would respond with empathy and integrity. An established set of team norms becomes a way to drive psychological safety because a team can insert behavior techniques like Inquire and Affirm into their team norms. Or, you can commit to disagreeing with each other's ideas and not attack the person as a way of setting healthy boundaries for conflict.

🧪 **CHALLENGE YOURSELF**

Does your team have an established set of team norms that help enhance psychological safety? If not, what steps can you take to kick off this process?

When I raise this leader's commitment with my clients, they sometimes sheepishly ask if it is too late—or simply weird—to add this if they've been leading an intact team for quite some time. The answer is simple: it is never too late to commit to a collaborative process of establishing team norms. You can simply say, "Team, we've been working well together, and it's occurred to me that we will benefit from having a set of team norms for how we interact, give feedback, and respond to challenging moments."

Leading your team in a brainstorming and ranking process for these kinds of norms often results in the leader learning a ton about their team's needs and priorities. Building a set of team norms can not only help the team bolster psychological safety, but it might also alert the leader to where future skill-building work is needed based on what emerges in the brainstorm. And remember, team norms should never become a stale artifact sitting in a cloud drive somewhere. Keep this as a living document. Revisit it with the team often, and reference it when making tough decisions or responding to feedback.

Wrapping Up: Getting Comfortable with Feeling Uncomfortable

I've sometimes heard leaders of large organizations try to engage and challenge their employees by calling for folks to ". . . get comfortable with feeling uncomfortable." I understand what they're asking for, and it often comes from a good place. Top leaders need their employees to

be able to navigate uncertainty and volatility in today's workforce as these have become normative conditions in our rapidly changing world. We also have a workforce with four generations of adults working alongside each other, and each of these generations brings a different perspective as to what a reasonable and positive work environment looks like. Amidst this mix of endless macro disruption and internal generational friction, I've listened to many executives gripe about wanting their people to ". . . toughen up and be okay with being uncomfortable."

While I can empathize with the desired outcome, I also see where we're missing the support to get there. Our ability to navigate discomfort is linearly tied to feeling safe enough to handle, discuss, and mitigate the discomfort. Whether we are thinking about a human instinct for survival or extensive research on change management in organizations, the same truism plays out: for humans to rise to their higher functions, safety is a precursor. Safety starts with physical safety, but the research on performance quickly challenges us to understand how fundamental psychological safety really is. To paraphrase Clark's model in service of the Alchemy of Talent, we must commit to making people feel included, safe to learn, safe to contribute, and safe to challenge if we want them to do the best work of their lives.

This does not mean, however, that psychological safety is about "babying" the workforce.

> *Safety does not eliminate discomfort. In fact, high levels of psychological safety unlock our ability to perform while feeling very uncomfortable.*

Similarly, psychological safety is not the same thing as "consensus culture"—where everyone must agree and tough decisions are not made. Conversely, high psychological safety primes a team for the "disagree and commit" approach to decision-making. Many executives call for a more robust culture of vocal disagreement amongst their teams (remember how friction makes things better?). They also call for team leaders to be able to commit to a course of action after eliciting productive disagreement. "Disagree and commit" may be an attractive method for an organization to move forward with excellence . . . but it cannot happen without high levels of psychological safety.

The Alchemy of Talent requires numerous catalysts to unlock the magic of peak performance. Psychological safety is foundational, but did you notice that the Clark model starts with something a bit different than safety? Before Learner Safety, Contributor Safety, or Challenger Safety comes something unexpected. Clark calls this first stage "Inclusion Safety" and describes it as being accepted and granted a shared identity by a group. The profound feeling of being included shows up broadly in the research on performance. We know what it feels like to be accepted for who we are and what it feels like to be excluded. As a team or organizational leader, it can feel like a lofty goal—or a lot of pressure—to make people feel truly included on your team. Lucky for us, we have a second Alchemy of Talent catalyst to help us get there: Belonging.

3

Catalyst: Belonging

There's a crisis of belonging in the US workforce. Through the disruptions of the last few years, we've seen the psychological health and overall well-being of employees drop dramatically.[1,2] As a result, employees are more likely than ever to switch jobs and take additional sick days to compensate. Even with a wealth of evidence that belonging is a key driver for employee and organizational success, many organizations do not have a plan in place to measure, generate, and sustain a sense of belonging for their workforce. In this chapter, I will explore how this powerful catalyst in the Alchemy of Talent works for teams and organizations, and how it can support the Case for Complexity.

But first, let me make it personal . . .

My journey of belonging started through a painful journey of not belonging. In 1986, when I was eight years old, my immigrant parents bought a house where they could afford one. It was a huge accomplishment for them after nearly two decades of hustling in North America. Our little townhouse happened to be in a border zone: a neighborhood right at the northern edge of the city of Chicago. Painting with a broad brush, if you headed south from my house, the community was largely Black, very low-resourced, and deeply affected by the 1980s crack epidemic and war on drugs. If you headed north from my house, you could bask under the shade of 100-year-old oak trees lining the quiet streets of Evanston, a relatively affluent North Shore suburb.

Demographically, this north/south divide tracked along the same race and class lines that are part of the broader American story, with the North Shore suburb far Whiter than the Chicago neighborhood that faced so many challenges. And, in the middle of all of this, there was me and my sister: two little Indian kids, taking the Chicago Transit Authority bus to school every day. Thinking back, my childhood experience of "diversity" is yet another poignant reminder that complexity alone does not generate better outcomes. My highly stratified community was definitely complex, but it was also a tense, painful place, haunted by inequity and hopelessness.

By the time I got to high school, the fault lines of race and class really began to shake, and I found myself spending most of my mental energy trying to stay safe. As one of the few Indian kids, I stood out and was the target of extended xenophobia and bullying. With two parents who worked in education, we didn't have the financial tailwinds to mix with the North Shore crowd of White kids. The Black kids in my immediate orbit had no particular love or tolerance for me . . . I was simply not Black. I hated being different and feeling both hyper-visible and invisible at the same time. My difference was frequently the source of anguish, and I couldn't wait to get through high school and escape from there.

My high school transcript isn't a particular point of pride in my life. I was an average student at best and often under-delivered against my potential. It was very difficult for me to be courageous, speak up, take healthy risks, and enjoy learning given the circumstances of my environment. I even found it difficult to just sit and focus on tough subjects like chemistry or algebra because I was unsafe, anxious, and lonely.

Fast forward . . .

A decade after I graduated high school, I worked at a university in the city of Chicago with a baccalaureate and master's degree from selective research institutions. My job at that time was to help design systems and programs to empower college students to persist and graduate, especially if they faced numerous structural disadvantages like being a first-generation college student or having to work full-time while pursuing their undergrad. I remember reading my first research paper on the concept of belonging, particularly because it related to student performance. The paper presented vast evidence that how students feel in a community, school, or team can make or break their academic performance. I was overwhelmed by how significant belonging was in student success.

The collective empirical study of belonging in education helped me understand my own journey. Without a strong sense of belonging in high school, I was unlikely to perform well academically. And, as I gained a better sense of belonging in college and grad school, my actual potential was able to shine through, and I was regularly at the top of my class. Beyond shedding light on my own journey, the research on belonging helped me design systems and programs that promoted strong student success outcomes for students who were normally at a high risk of not persisting through to graduation. In education, belonging is seen as rocket fuel for student success.

Does the same hold true for employees and their success?

Knowing It

Imagine a space in your life where you are truly able to be yourself. This could be with your family, a faith community, or your team at work. When you're in this environment and around these people, you feel more relaxed, able to think clearly, able to bounce back from mistakes . . . You're closer to being your best self. When you're in this space, compared to other spaces, you feel like you can "take off the mask" of performance, such as performing perfection or performing constant optimism. For some, this might be the mask of performing culturally to fit into a culture that is different than their own home culture. Being able to take off the mask of performance allows you to breathe, relax your shoulders, and just be. Imagine this space, community, family . . .that feeling you now have is a sense of belonging.

The definition of belonging that I use most frequently when considering EX comes from the researchers at Coqual.[3] This definition of belonging is highly validated through broad research, and it resonates with people on a human level, thereby passing my behavioral science smell test! Employees have a high sense of belonging when they feel:

- **Seen:** they feel recognized, rewarded, and respected by colleagues.
- **Connected:** they have positive, authentic social interactions with peers, managers, and senior leaders.
- **Supported:** coworkers give them what they need to get work done and live a full life.
- **Proud:** their work and organization feel aligned with their values, vision, and purpose.

On the flip side, humans can experience a lack of social belonging as literal pain.

Some scientists[4] think that our need for social belonging is hardwired into our evolutionary biology. Since we have historically relied on social belonging as a survival mechanism (e.g., human children cannot survive harsh conditions without the help of adults), our brains appear to have evolved to experience a lack of social belonging through a pain response. In neuroscience research labs, the brain imaging for low belonging matches the imaging for a person experiencing pain. This may be an evolutionary reflex to alert us to the historic dangers of isolation. We can all relate to moments of not belonging in some space or period of our lives and how difficult it is to show your true potential when you feel isolated.

In my work with engineering teams at software companies, I often hear a theme emerge from women and people of color. They speak about struggling to belong when they don't feel normalized in the team environment due to being deeply under-represented on these

teams. The day-to-day battle with loneliness can inter-fere with their peak performance and reduce their resil-ience. The theme emerged so often in my focus groups and one-on-one connections at software companies that I started calling the phenomenon the "loneliness of only-ness." When you're the only one, it can be chal-lenging to gain a robust sense of belonging.

Belonging as a Catalyst for Performance

The workplace has a long way to go to understand and invest in belonging. In many organizations, it is still treated as a nice-to-have when there is plenty of evi-dence that it is a must-have. During 2021, the US work-force experienced a huge shift: people left their jobs in unprecedented numbers, often without having another job lined up already. Pundits referred to this trend as the Great Resignation or the Great Attrition. McKinsey[5] con-ducted a large study of the workforce during this period of churn and found that 54 percent of workers studied associated quitting their jobs with not feeling valued at work. Belonging, or not belonging, shows up as a leading indicator in data on voluntary attrition.

Conversely, researchers at BetterUp[6] found that workers who reported a high sense of belonging were 50 percent less likely to leave, 75 percent less prone to taking sick days, and 56 percent more likely to indicate successful performance when compared to employees who indicated a low sense of workplace belonging. Furthermore, employees with a high sense of belonging also had much higher net promoter scores, resulting in their willingness to promote their employer brand externally and recommend their place of employment to their network.

These are powerful correlations for any organization that relies on its employees to drive their success! To take their research one step further, BetterUp scientists conducted a controlled experiment to assess the impact of not belonging, and they consistently found that excluded study participants were significantly less likely to work for the benefit of their team. So, even in an organization where attrition is not a big risk, we can see how a low sense of belonging is still a threat.

Belonging can drive peak performance when it is present, but its absence can sow the seeds of under-performance.

The Alchemy of Talent: The Value of Belonging for Complex Teams

Now that you have a working definition of belonging and evidence that it can drive individual, team, and company performance, let's go back and consider the Case for Complexity. When organizations attempt to harness the productive power of friction by assembling diverse teams, we know that we need the catalyst of psychological safety to help individuals and teams experience this friction

safely and productively. You'll recall that Clark's model of psychological safety reminds us that the foundation for feeling the full spectrum of psychological safety is to feel included. Belonging—or feeling seen, connected, supported, and proud—is a key driver of inclusion. Investing in systems and behaviors that promote belonging for all your employees sets the stage for strong feelings of inclusion, which is required for psychological safety. The catalyst of belonging works in concert with the catalyst of psychological safety to create the Alchemy of Talent on complex teams.

Spotting It: Scanning Your Environment

My theory of change has a middle step between understanding a concept (Knowing It) and committing to behaviors that advance it (Doing It). Talent leaders benefit immensely from conducting quick environmental scans to take stock of how an EX construct is showing up—or not—in the unique context of their workplace. All meaning is relative to context, so taking the ideas from this book and localizing them in your organizational context is a valuable exercise. Concepts like psychological safety or belonging may manifest differently in a sports team, a manufacturing plant, or a software engineering team. I encourage talent leaders to use a mapping template for belonging to chart out what good and great looks like in their workplace. Here's an example:

Examples of Belonging at Work		
	Good	Great
Individual who belongs	Actively refers open jobs in their organization to qualified colleagues in their network.	Able to take a calculated risk and stumble without doubting their fit or future in the organization.
Team that belongs	Team members are encouraged to retain their uniqueness while being accepted as part of the team.	Team members are given frequent opportunities to contribute to key decisions that affect their work experience and outcomes.
Organization that invests in belonging	Complexity of leadership in the organization reflects complexity found in the entry level and mid level of the organization.	Organization ritualizes and invests in frequent recognition of employee efforts and successes.

Doing It: Generating and Sustaining Belonging at Work

Just like we did with the catalyst of psychological safety, it's imperative that we go beyond knowing what belonging is and being able to spot it in our work contexts. We need skills and behaviors that make this happen for our teams! Tactics for generating and sustaining belonging for a team can differ from creating environments and systems for belonging across the entire organization. To illustrate this point, I will share a team-level best practice, as well as an organizational approach.

 CHALLENGE YOURSELF

Take a minute to think about the team you work on. What does your team do well to generate belonging? What's something that could be better?

Ritualizing Recognition: Belonging at the Team Level

In one of my university leadership roles, I had regular contact with a board of trustees committee. I remember going through a particularly difficult semester where I was tasked with managing several high-risk free speech issues on campus. The project took tremendous effort and complex negotiations with everyone from legal counsel to student activists to police leadership. At the end of the semester, the institution had successfully navigated three high-visibility free speech challenges, while many of our peer institutions had experienced complete meltdowns during similar moments.

As the semester wrapped up, I was exhausted and ready for a much-needed break! A month after the semester ended, I was at a gathering with several board committee members and they came over to thank me for the work I did during the semester. Except, they couldn't remember any of the specifics, so their praise came out as general platitudes: "Congrats on doing a great job!" Their attempt at recognition was both late and vague . . . and it had exactly the opposite effect of what they intended. I left that event feeling deflated. I could have used the pat on the back while over-clocking under intense scrutiny for fifteen weeks. Their lack of clear details in the praise gave me the distinct impression that they didn't actually know what I'd accomplished, which made me feel even worse.

In their attempt to help me feel seen, the board members unintentionally made me feel unseen, which lowered my sense of belonging. Recognition is a potent tool to address both the "feeling seen" and "feeling proud" elements of belonging for your team members. When I engage with team leaders and ask them about the science of recognition, or what model they use to ritualize recognition, I mostly get blank stares. This tells me that the workplace has a long way to go to maximize the power of this tool! My experience appears to be reflected across the workplace, with only 34 percent of employees reporting that their workplace has a recognition program in a recent study by Workhuman and Gallup.[7]

I love the simplicity of Gostick and Elton's model of recognition,[8] drawn from their extensive research on EX and recognition outcomes. For recognition to have the maximum effect on driving employee belonging it needs to be frequent, specific, and timely.

What does a recognition model really look like?

- **Frequent:** People need frequent acknowledgment that their work matters and their successes are visible to the team leader. Saving all your praise for an end-of-year dinner is counterproductive.
- **Specific:** People want to know that their manager has a precise understanding of their work and why they were successful. A generalized "keep up the good work" can be alienating as it may communicate that the manager is unaware of the team member's specific contributions.
- **Timely:** A team member who has gone the extra mile on a project needs to hear a precise "thank you" from their leader close to the time when the extra effort was required. Recognition of extraordinary work that happens a long time after the specific achievement has a diminished effect on employee morale and sense of satisfaction.

What would it look like if this recognition model had been in place when I was handling the large, complex project for the university? Let's wave our magic wand and imagine an alternate ending to that story:

. . . As the semester wrapped up, I was exhausted and ready for a much-needed break! I knew I'd done well because I'd received several timely notes recognizing my skillful leadership from board members at key project milestones. Before leaving the office that final Friday, my supervisor knocked on my door and said, "Do you have a minute?" I invited her in, and she told me, "I know this was a tough project, requiring you to balance tough deadlines with plenty of workplace politics. I'm really proud of how you handled yourself and the whole team is shining because of your hard work." I left for semester break feeling proud of where I worked, valued for my efforts, and eager to contribute to big projects in the future.

🧪 CHALLENGE YOURSELF

Consider a time that you've felt truly recognized by a manager that didn't involve a promotion or a raise. How and when did this recognition happen? What elements of frequent, specific, and timely showed up in this example?

In my work with team leaders, I ask them to look back on times they felt truly recognized at work and identify what elements of the recognition model show up. I also ask them to think of recognition as a ritual. Rituals happen often, and the more we observe them, the more natural and habitual they become. Managers who excel at generating and sustaining team belonging make recognition a habit, and their teams feel seen and proud as a result.

Making Belonging Part of the Organizational DNA

A single team leader can generate belonging on their team. While this is absolutely worth doing, organizations that leave this up to individual leaders risk an uneven EX. When I consult with talent leaders at organizations with extreme peaks and valleys of belonging, they often report issues that need to be avoided, if possible: feelings of "haves and have-nots" between high-belonging and low-belonging teams; attempts at internal transfers to get out of low-belonging teams onto high-belonging teams; and high levels of regrettable attrition across the organization. It can be transformational to invest in *organizational* belonging by leveraging skills and systems as part of an enterprise strategy to make belonging part of your organizational DNA.

Here's an example of how an HR leadership team could map out potential investment opportunities at two levels to create an enterprise belonging campaign. The columns represent the four categories from the definition of belonging presented earlier in this chapter. The rows are broken into two separate categories. First, skill-building tactics require a focus on employee competency development and skill acquisition. The second row offers examples of tactics that require systemic change, complex implementation, and broad executive buy-in. These system-based approaches to belonging may have a heavier lift, but they also consistently show up in the best practice literature on world-class organizational belonging! When it comes to belonging as DNA, the juice is worth the squeeze to work at both the skill level and the system level.

Integrating Belonging into the DNA of Your Organization		
Organizational Belonging	Seen	Connected
Skill Building	Teach leaders how to ritualize recognition for their teams (see above).	Upskill leaders on the behavioral science of mutuality to drive connection on complex teams. (If you're scratching your head, just wait until the next chapter on the catalyst of connection to find out!)
System Building	Annual social norming campaign. Focus on a community that struggles to be seen and invite leaders and employees at all levels in the organization to share their story through digital campaign to normalize this experience. Examples: veterans sharing their story of challenge and triumph at work, people with visible/ invisible disabilities sharing their pathway to success at work.	Design ERGs that are engines of connection. Employee resource groups can be designed to drive a multitude of outcomes and one strong application of an ERG is to enhance connection across the organization, by allowing people to join affinity communities. Research on ERG best practices consistently shows that employees who are actively involved in an ERG report higher sense of belonging than uninvolved employees, and this is in part because of the ERG serving as a source of connection.

Integrating Belonging into the DNA of Your Organization		
Organizational Belonging	**Supported**	**Proud**
Skill Building	Have managers add a "battery check" indicator to all of their directs' weekly reports. This is a simple way for team members to be able to share that they may be running low on "battery life" and then the manager can inquire and find ways to support—before full burnout sets in.	Teach leaders how to bring organizational values to life by connecting them to each team's work and "why." For employees to feel proud, they need frequent reminders of how their effort contributes to the big picture wins and advances the organization's values.
System Building	Provide your employees with the opportunity to have a career, not a job. The difference between the job someone has today and a career is found in the opportunity to learn and grow within the organization. Investing in skill and competency development that allows for internal mobility is a key way to increase the feeling of systemic support.	Employees feel proud when their organization is committed to fairness. Investing in annual pay equity audits and being transparent about improvements from these processes can transmit organizational values and commitments to fairness in ways that increase employee pride. People want to work in organizations where they feel aligned to purpose and values.

Wrapping Up: On Chickens and Eggs

For individuals, teams, and whole organizations, a sense of belonging is a catalyst to unlock the Alchemy of Talent. As you explore broader research and best practice writing on belonging, you may notice that it is often paired with the word "inclusion" or, more recently, it shows up at the end of the acronym D.E.I.B. (diversity, equity, inclusion, and belonging). There is a causal relationship between belonging and inclusion that is helpful for leaders to understand. One of these concepts is the chicken; the other is the egg.

Belonging is the input (egg) and inclusion is the outcome (chicken). If you are seeking broad, robust inclusion for your team or workforce (and you should be after reading Chapter 2!), then invest in the catalyst of belonging to produce the outcome of inclusion. Stacking more letters onto DEI to make DEIB can be confusing for leaders. Diversity, equity, and inclusion are three outcomes. They are the result of organizations investing in policies, systems, and employee skills across the entire workforce. Individual team leaders that I coach often struggle with what they can do to increase a mega factor like inclusion. I tell them to focus on belonging. The concept is more relatable; the tactics are easier to deploy at the team level. And, when a sense of belonging increases, so does a sense of inclusion. While inclusion is bigger than just belonging, people's sense of belonging has a significant impact on whether they feel included in a team or organization. When I work with leaders, I often clarify what tools are available (inputs), and what aggregate factors we're pursuing (outcomes). Leaders I advise have found it clear and valuable to see belonging as something we must turn up the volume on if we want our workforce to feel included.

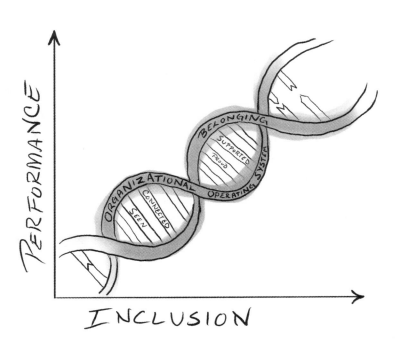

While we're on the subject of chickens and eggs, you may have noticed that a condition for belonging is feeling connected. Connection happens to be our third and final catalyst in the Alchemy of Talent. While connection is definitely a part of feeling a genuine sense of belonging, it also has broader implications that are particularly valuable for teams and organizations navigating change and uncertainty. Let's see how connection factors into unlocking the power of complex teams in Chapter 4.

4

Catalyst: Connection

Many organizations now think of their approach to work in three ways: onsite, remote, or hybrid. The great disruption of 2020, the COVID-19 pandemic, changed many norms in the world of work. While some workplace adjustments were made from sheer necessity in the early days of the pandemic, by 2022, executives struggled to find the right balance between the organizational benefits of onsite work and the individual employee's desire for remote work. I see this as a productive tension in a competitive labor marketplace. Companies are now experimenting with myriad models of how to strike this balance: what tools to use to enhance collaboration for distributed teams, how to train leaders specifically to lead remote workers, and what to focus on when teams are actually onsite.

Connection is desperately needed across the EX, and it may be one of the most neglected factors. Research on how connected employees feel to each other and to their organization consistently points to the same conclusions: highly connected employees stay at the organization longer, do better work, and refer open roles in the organization to their network.[1] This was true before the health disruption of 2020,[2] and it remains true now. The strong human desire "to be known" in life shows up at work, but the unresolved story of onsite, remote, and hybrid work arrangements leaves team connection swinging in the wind. As organizations apply greater intentionality to their overall workplace strategy, we have the golden opportunity to centralize team connection in our planning.

This chapter will demonstrate how connection functions as a catalyst in the Alchemy of Talent and why it may be the jet fuel we need for the workforce right now. Whether you are an architect of your organization's overall EX or a team leader committed to helping your team succeed, this chapter will empower you to act with intention and unlock peak performance for your employees.

The Team that Plays Together . . .

Looking back on fifteen years of leading teams in large, complex organizations, one of the teams I've felt most connected to is a group of people that I never met in person while we were on the team! And based on the conditions that got us onto this team, you'd never bet on us forming a connected, high-performance group.

In the first year of the COVID-19 pandemic, I led a multi-functional team of HR practitioners at a global software company. We were remote due to our closed offices and distributed across time zones and countries. We were complex (see Chapter 1) across numerous inherent and acquired traits like age, race, sexual orientation, skillset, job level, and domain expertise. I was recruited as an external hire into a newly created C-level role that brought previously disparate units together in a new center of excellence. I was also tasked with bringing several new hires to the team. To sum it up: we were remote, different, and deeply unfamiliar with one another. On top of all of that, we were all navigating an unprecedented disruption to the very fabric of work and life while attempting to become a cohesive team.

How did we go from a balkanized collection of individuals to a highly connected team?

A few actions helped us immensely. First, we built time into each weekly staff meeting to share about our lives. We used a "Wired, Tired, Inspired" sharing ritual each week to encourage people to share a recent win or positive moment (wired), something that was challenging for them (tired), and something they were looking forward to (inspired). There was no single experience of this agenda item that magically generated connection, but the aggregate effect was clear. Over time, we grew to know and understand each other better because of the consistent sharing of the big and small things that affected our lives.

We also normalized failure by ritualizing how we shared our mistakes. I realized early on that we were going to have a lot of "oops" and "ouch" moments as a team. We came from different units and backgrounds and were tasked with a lot of brand-new implementations: building programs and products from scratch. There is no innovation without failure, but fear of failure must be intentionally managed (see Chapter 2). During our weekly meeting, I created a ritual called "Fantastic Fudge Ups" where anyone could share something that did not go as planned and what they learned from it. And, since I knew that we weren't at a high level of trust in the beginning, I often went first during this ritual to remind the team of my vulnerability and to inspire confidence that they too could participate without fear of shame. Like the Wired, Tired, and Inspired ritual, this weekly check-in on failure moved us incrementally toward connection by building vulnerability and trust in the group.

Finally, we played together. We used to say, "The team that plays together stays together," and we found ways, once a month, to play together. Sometimes we met up on a Friday afternoon, virtually, and played online games that were quite silly but tons of fun. These games imitated popular household games like Charades or Pictionary. Even delivered in virtual meeting platforms we could collaborate and play as a distributed team. Sometimes, when we had a little budget, we would use a vendor to do an activity together—like have sushi-making or pottery-painting kits shipped to our houses. We would all log into a teambuilding meeting where an instructor would lead us in a low-stress activity that would leave us joking, laughing, and learning together. But, as the leader, I knew how important these times were for us and I worked to create both budget and capacity for us to treat this time like "work" and to commit to it consistently once a month.

In leading that team, we developed a strong sense of connection to each other and the team as a whole. This didn't mean we experienced problem-free bliss . . . but it allowed us to productively confront and conquer the problems that always occur on complex teams at work.

I love to cook, and I often notice a finished dish is much tastier than any of its individual ingredients. These dishes often involve a sauce that unlocks the magic of the recipe. For our team, connection was our secret sauce. It was a catalyst for resilience and performance at a particularly challenging time for the workforce. For me, as the leader of this team, the dissonance between the actual conditions of our lives (isolated during a global pandemic) and the feeling on the team (connected, trusting, energized) gave me a lot to think about. Is connection the secret sauce for the workforce in general?

Knowing It

When adults think back on how they made their closest lifelong friends, they often identify specific conditions that led to making a best friend. Social network analysis researchers have been fascinated by how people form and maintain friendships for decades, and there is growing evidence pointing to high-quality relationships as a driver of long-term health and happiness. Behavioral psychologists who study the phenomenon of connection describe this concept as a feeling of closeness between two people. While connection in our personal lives has been an enduring subject of research, there is growing and much-needed interest in this factor at work! Closeness, or connection, is also a workplace tool rooted in science and data and tied to optimal team performance. But how relevant is it for employers and for the basic understanding of how people function?

My favorite study of the power of connection in human lives is the Harvard Study of Adult Development, often referred to as the Grant Study.[3] In 1938, researchers at Harvard began one of the longest uninterrupted studies of adult life by examining a cohort of Harvard students and non-Harvard students. Over time, the researchers scaled the cohort of study participants to include the offspring of the initial study participants. Eighty-six years later, this study of human health and happiness is ongoing.

The study found that high-quality relationships are closely correlated with our long-term health and happiness. This finding cuts across numerous meaningful demographic factors pointing to the universality of the human desire for connection.

No matter what way you cut it, the evidence always screams the same thing: humans are social beings.

Connection and Workplace Performance

Our desire for connection as social beings is not limited to our personal lives.

Organizations that study employee engagement have asked about social connection at work for years and it always shows up as a significant factor in employee retention, productivity, and net promoter scores.[4] When Gallup first added the item "I have a best friend at work" to their industry-standard employee engagement survey, everyone from corporate executives to the news media mocked this as an unimportant factor. Over the years that followed, the data challenged this view.[5] Employees who reported having a best friend at work were more likely to be engaged with customers and internal partners, were more productive, and were more supportive of a safe workplace environment.

Another way to understand the power of connection in driving resilient, high-performing teams is to look qualitatively at the practices of organizations that outperform, especially under tremendous pressure. This is the focus of Daniel Coyle's multi-year journey, following elite teams in a multitude of sectors.[6] Coyle finds that, on elite teams, leaders are consistently the first to initiate vulnerability. They take the leap of admitting what they don't know or confessing a mistake they made. Surprisingly, leaders of elite, intensely competitive teams can put their pride and ego aside and own it when they make mistakes or simply don't have the answers! This leap of vulnerability elicits a sense of connection from the team as team members feel closer to a leader who trusts them enough to name the unknown or their own mistakes. For elite teams, a sense of connection sets the stage for psychological safety, risk-taking, and learning from failure, which all contribute to their consistently high performance.

Three Key Drivers of Connection

Just because humans are social beings that desire closeness with others doesn't mean we necessarily understand the mechanics of creating and sustaining this closeness in complex, diverse team environments. In my work coaching leaders, I've found it necessary to unpack the drivers behind connection before moving into the specific skills and behaviors that increase connection on the team. Having a strong understanding of the science of connection will allow you to lead in ways that increase connection on your team.

1. Commonality: connection through similarity.

Social network researchers have observed the powerful role of commonality in driving interpersonal connection for decades. This shows up in our personal lives if we think about our closest friends. There's a good chance that you and a best friend found several things you had in common, especially in the beginning stages of your friendship. At work, finding something in common with a teammate is an accessible tactic for building connection, but it relies on an on-ramp that is difficult to access if you're on a complex team.

 CHALLENGE YOURSELF

Do you have an intentional strategy for team connection at work? After reading Chapter 1, what are the dangers of over-relying on commonality for complex teams?

Imagine that you're on a global team and you are the only team member from your country. Your culture, experiences, native language, and faith set you apart from your team. Relying on commonality as your only tool for building connection would be a fool's errand. Most leaders in large, complex organizations often reveal to me that they do not have an intentional strategy to generate and sustain connection. This tells me that they are unconsciously relying on commonality to drive connection.

When I worked as a chief diversity officer for numerous large organizations, I often observed two simultaneous phenomena at work: first, the organization would commit to myriad strategies and tactics that increased complexity across teams; second, team cohesion would often drop as a result. What was happening?!

The challenge facing organizations that actually invest in assembling teams with tremendous built-in friction through inherent and acquired traits is that commonality becomes less useful in driving team connection. Team members and leaders in these settings often find themselves feeling de-skilled in the face of complexity. Diverse, complex teams require a considerable investment in leader upskilling to harness the team's compositional difference as a strength. We should celebrate teams that become less homogenous due to intentional effort, but we also must support and invest in team leaders. They need more tools than commonality to build and sustain connection across their team.

2. Mutuality: connection through reciprocal trust.

Scientists who study human social networks have examined how people form lasting connection when they do not share an initial set of common traits or experiences.[7] When I think about my career, I can observe several workplace relationships that were quite close, but I didn't have much in common with a coworker. When I reflect on how we achieved connection, there is generally a process of having to work together on a tough project, and during this effort, we had to rely on each other, support one another during mistakes, and experience the joy of shared success. This process of building connection without trait-based commonality is called mutuality, and it is built on trust and reciprocity.

Mutuality describes the way that connection can build over time between people who take an interest in each other's careers and support one another through challenges. Mutuality has several important components, two of which I find to be central in sustaining workplace connection: trust and reciprocity. When a pair of coworkers has to navigate a shared challenge, one coworker can lean into the relationship by sending a trust signal to the other coworker. A trust signal is an act of vulnerability such as saying, "I'm nervous about the pitch meeting because I'm really great with data analytics, but public speaking is my kryptonite!" or, during a project, if one colleague says, "I need to let you know that I'm behind on my portion of the work because my daughter had an ear infection over the last few days."

These moments of truth require vulnerability on the part of the sharer . . . but they also open the door to receiving trust signals and choosing to send one back. Let's see how each of these trust signals can be met with a responding trust signal:

> **Trust signal A:** "I'm nervous about the pitch meeting because I'm really great with data analytics but public speaking is my kryptonite!"

> **Response signal A:** "Thanks for letting me know. I totally get how public speaking can be anxiety-producing. How about I pretend to be the audience and you practice the pitch opener with me until you feel comfortable?"

> **Trust signal B:** "I need to let you know that I'm behind on my portion of the work because my daughter had an ear infection over the last few days."

> **Response signal B:** "I'm so sorry to hear about your daughter. That sounds tough. Why don't I build those slides for you so we can get back on track with our timeline and meet this upcoming deadline?"

In the language of mutuality, this response signal establishes reciprocity and sets off a positive feedback loop between two people that can generate a strong sense of connection over time.

The magic of mutuality is in how the response to the trust signal generates closeness between people.[8]

3. Novelty: connection through fun.

It might seem odd to be reading about something like novelty in a book on high-performing teams, but the axiom "Teams that play together stay together" actually shows up in the research! Now, before you buy a ping-pong table for the office, it is important to clarify that novelty can also be found in work-based tasks.

When I am unpacking the research on novelty for leaders, I often describe novel experiences as moments that are less familiar and moderately challenging. If tasks are extremely challenging, our sense of novelty generally decreases. Similarly, if an experience is far too familiar, it rarely produces a sense of novelty. But workplace experiences that combine the right amount of challenge and familiarity can unlock a strong sense of connection for the people participating.

Psychologists explain the math of novelty through effort justification: people attribute greater value to things and processes that they have worked on.[9] Think about novel work-based experiences like hack-a-thons in software companies or product pitch competitions for sales teams with company executives playing "Shark Tank" roles. These experiences balance challenge and familiarity to provide experiences that allow employees to grow closer while doing something that may benefit the organization as a whole.

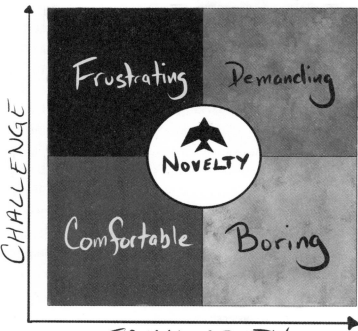

I often bring up the science of novelty with leaders who tell me they are leading a team through a particularly difficult and volatile time for their organization. When I ask them about connection, they sometimes share that they plan on hosting a nice dinner at the next offsite/retreat to help people feel more connected. As a foodie, it hurts me to say this but . . . nice dinners do not harness the power of novelty. Sitting in a restaurant and ordering food is actually a very familiar task, even if the cuisine is new to the diner. In a team setting, the dinner seating arrangements often result in each person just speaking to the two or three people seated closest to them. The process of dining together does not tap into the psychology of effort to generate connection. In these moments, I try to nudge leaders to be intentional about having a connection experience before or after the dinner, such as doing an escape room together, going axe-throwing, or inviting in a facilitator to lead the group through some fast-paced icebreakers that leverage the science of novelty and connection.

While these experiences may take more effort to plan than a nice dinner, they also will pay dividends for the team as a stronger sense of connection functions as a catalyst for team cohesion and performance.

The Alchemy of Talent: Connection on Complex Teams

Companies that build complex teams to capture the productive power of friction are often met with lower team cohesion due to the lack of easy commonality as a driver of connection. Skillful leaders can employ mutuality and novelty to generate lasting connection on their complex teams. The highly connected team, with loads of built-in acquired and inherent diversity, is better positioned to achieve antifragile design in their pursuit of the organization's goals.

Connection is a particularly useful catalyst in the Alchemy of Talent right now, at a time when disruption fatigue is setting in for the global workforce. Highly connected teams can adapt to volatility and uncertainty better due to unit cohesion, which increases team resilience.

In my work with organizations responding to numerous changes, leaders often raise the issue of wanting a more resilient workforce that is ready for the inevitability of disruption in our world. It has been clear to me for years that connection, along with psychological safety and belonging, are needed to unlock the magic of performance. The recent past specifically challenged teams to navigate a pandemic, global activism, macroeconomic volatility, geopolitical conflict, and now generative AI. Connection shows up repeatedly as the third catalyst to help complex teams outperform in the rapid pace of disruption and uncertainty that are hallmarks of the 21st century.

Spotting It

As I did in Chapters 2 and 3, it can be helpful to map out what connection looks like in the workplace. Leaders can use this guidance to scan their environment and workplace context and identify where connection is happening and where there are opportunities to improve.

Examples of Highly Connected Teams		
	Good	**Great**
The Connected Leader	Models vulnerability for their teams.	Ritualizes connection activities in regular meetings.
The Connected Team Member	Makes an effort to build relationships, not just "get the work done."	Gives vulnerability and responds with trust to generate closeness with coworkers.
The Connected Organization	Invests budget and effort for connection, particularly during times of volatility and uncertainty.	Develops an enterprise connection strategy that fits their model of work (onsite, hybrid, remote).

Doing It

For our first two catalysts, psychological safety and belonging, we didn't stop at becoming familiar with the ideas; we dug into the skills that make this happen for your team! You know what connection is, why it matters for complex, high-performance teams, and what psychological drivers are in the leader toolbox. Here are two immediate actions you as leaders can take that apply what you've learned to turn up the volume on connection for your team.

It Starts with You

The science of mutuality is clear: trust and reciprocation can create lasting connection between coworkers, even if they don't have a lot in common. Leaders I coach often want this for their teams and ask what they can do to make mutuality go viral at work. My answer is that this process starts with you.

If you remember what we know about psychological safety, team members are unlikely to take risks at work that they don't see normalized by their leader. Mutuality requires vulnerability: someone has to initiate the trust loop by signaling vulnerability. Asking the team to do this without modeling it as a leader is weak leadership.

Think of a time when you've witnessed a competent leader show up with vulnerability. How did you feel at this moment? Did you, or anyone else on the team, do something in response that signaled, "We see you as being vulnerable, we respect this, we trust you?"

When I keynote and introduce the idea that leaders must go first with vulnerability, there's often a bipolar reaction in the audience. I can sort the audience vibe by tracking the bloom of reactions across the room. One group will have knowing smiles on their faces. These are the folks who have been using this superpower for some time and know how potent it is in unlocking peak performance for their team. I can also see another set of faces . . .these people wear an expression like I've just asked them to jump into a freezing pool of water: apprehension and skepticism! I can empathize with this latter group. Many workplaces still normalize a distant, robotic form of leadership where the leader manages the team's productivity and attempts to signal perfection in all tasks. As much as the research on effective leadership has challenged this outdated model for decades, I appreciate that it still exists, and we have to be strategic about how we frame and deploy vulnerability.

In coaching top executives, I have found two truths that require emphasis if a leader is going to adopt vulnerability as a driver of mutuality for their team: vulnerability isn't at war with competence,[10] and vulnerability scales from small to big.

First, I address the misnomer that vulnerability and competence are somehow in a tug-of-war with each other. So many executives have a mental model that puts these two key ideas in a contest rather than framing vulnerability and competence as equally necessary. The research on transformational leadership repeatedly points to top-performing leaders as both highly competent and vulnerable with their teams. A leader who errs too far on the side of vulnerability or competence risks under-performing in their role. I often use this kind of image to map the risks of not balancing vulnerability with competence:

I've found it helpful to illustrate that all vulnerability with low competence is just not effective, and conversely, all competence with no vulnerability risks a lack of followership from your team!

The second truth that helps leaders initiate vulnerability is the guidance that vulnerability scales from small to big. Leaders should not feel pressure to take massive risks in front of their team as some moonshot attempt to catalyze mutuality! Just like any skill, leaders should practice vulnerability at work by first taking small steps. For some leaders who are brand new to this approach, this could mean starting a Monday morning meeting

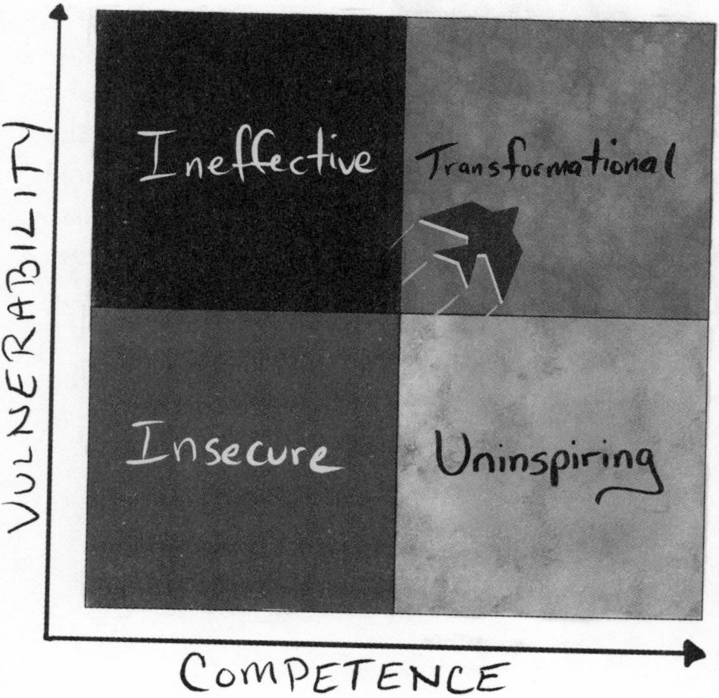

Ineffective
Transformational
Insecure
Uninspiring
VULNERABILITY
COMPETENCE

with a direct report by sharing a little bit about what they did over the weekend and then asking their team members how their weekends were. Or, if the whole team is navigating a frustrating set of changes, a leader could attempt a moment of strategic transparency by starting the meeting with, "I know this has been a frustrating period of change for our team. Personally, there have been moments where I've wanted to throw my hands up and give up. But I keep reminding myself why we're making this change . . ." This kind of vulnerability helps the team connect to the leader through shared empathy and requires minimal risk on the leader's part. By starting small with vulnerability, I've watched even C-suite executives move from uninspiring to transformational leadership.

Here are two common applications of vulnerability that leaders can use to drive mutuality and connection in their teams:

Vulnerability Behavior	The Common Mistake	Driving Connection
Name the Unknown	During times of uncertainty, leaders can feel pressure to "have all the answers." This is a mistake as it can lead you to avoid answering your team's questions with the honest answer, "I don't know." When leaders avoid naming the unknown, they decrease trust as team members can suspect the leader is hoarding relevant information.	When leaders take the courage to share that they do not have the answer to a pressing question from their team, it sends a signal of vulnerability that allows the team to respond with a signal of trust. The team that says, "Thanks for being honest. It's good to know that you don't have the answer right now," is expressing reciprocity with the leader. This response starts the loop that increases connection over time.
Own Mistakes	Leaders will make mistakes, as will members of their team. If leaders feel pressure to "be perfect," it can result in them avoiding publicly owning mistakes that the team is aware of. Avoiding ownership signals to the team that accountability is only top-down on the team. It lowers trust as team members conclude that the leader is not operating with integrity.	Leaders can signal vulnerability when they get the team together and name a mistake that they made, what they learned from it, and how they will correct going forward. This bid for trust goes out to the group and does two things: it models and invites psychological safety, and it allows the group to send a response signal back. The team that responds, "We appreciate you taking ownership. We get it because we make mistakes too," is sending a powerful signal of trust back to the leader. This loop increases connection on the team.

Ritualizing Connection for Distributed Teams

Distributed teams are now normal across many sectors of the workforce. When a team lives in a multitude of places, it can be more challenging for a team leader to generate and sustain a sense of connection for the team. The old model of relying on "the office" as a site of connection—one that capitalizes on coffee breaks and water cooler conversations—no longer serves the distributed team leader. When I'm coaching leaders in this situation, I offer the idea of "team rituals." A ritual is something that happens on a regular cadence that people can expect and even look forward to. Here are a few examples of connection rituals that you can adopt with your team:

- **Five Minutes of Fame:** This gratitude ritual leverages the science of recognition to drive team connection. Set aside five minutes at the start of every team meeting to allow team members to give each other shout-outs for things that went well, team members that went above and beyond, or a moment where someone was uniquely compassionate. Leaders can kick off this ritual by going first and role-modeling the behavior. Note: leaders should be aware that some team members may not get recognized for accomplishments because they are quiet or work behind the scenes. The leader should use their voice to recognize these individuals.

- **"I See You" Notes:** On distributed teams you cannot rely on the co-location of the office to provide easy moments to check in on your team members, give folks a pat on the back after a strong performance in a meeting, or follow up when someone has had a sick kid at home. Connection is about feeling close, even if we are apart. Leaders can foster connection by making a fifteen-minute appointment on their calendars, once a week, to be intentional about sending one or two people on their team a note about something that they want to acknowledge or check in on. This note can be over email, instant messaging, or even a card in the mail. These tiny nudges add up over time to a strong sense of closeness and connection without costing the leader much time or any budget.

- **Design for Silly:** Team leaders can ask their team to help think through ways to add levity and connection to a once-a-month team meeting using a variety of icebreakers or online games. Allowing the team to share their ideas on activities they've experienced before, or that they may particularly enjoy, creates a bottom-up sense of ownership when the team participates in these monthly rituals at the start of a meeting. Novel experiences can be low to no cost and optimized for virtual meetings through a variety of technology tools these days that offer teams small games they can play in a meeting as well. These investments are particularly meaningful during times of heightened stress and uncertainty.

Anthropologists and historians observe that humans use rituals to navigate times of uncertainty and change. Throughout history, we have found ways to mark the calendar with regular moments of meaning and connection that help us make sense of each other and our own lives. In the timeline of the post-industrial workplace, the notion of distributed teams is still quite new. Our leadership practices have not caught up with this approach to work. Many organizations have left "the office" behind without replacing the rituals that were tied to everyone working together in the same physical place. Team members on distributed teams often report a lower sense of connection to their team and organization, and this can undermine their ability to perform consistently at a high level. Ritualizing connection is a smart move for leaders that want to build and sustain a high-performing, distributed team.

Wrapping Up: On High-Water Marks

I recently chatted with a CEO/founder of a five-year-old company. Strong execution and brilliant timing have led this organization to grow from a starting team of three to now 350 employees. When I asked this CEO about the early days at the company, he quickly reflected, "Boy, we worked so hard in the beginning." But he had a wistful smile on his face that contrasted with the words of his statement. Curious, I asked him to tell me more about that time. He immediately launched into a story about working with his small team in the London office until late at night, and one person grabbed pizza and drinks for the group. They sat around the office at ten p.m., eating slices and sipping beverages and laughing about the week.

In talking about his company, this CEO could have shared any number of reflections with me that would be more "heroic" than the story he told. He could have talked about landing their first round of VC funding. He could have talked about signing their first Fortune 100 client. But no surprise to me, he talked about sitting in the office with a few people sharing a meal after a week of hard work.

This theme surfaces in so many conversations I've had with top organizational leaders. When asked about the high-water mark of their careers, the stories are most often not grandiose. They aren't about the big payday or winning the top award at work. Most often they are moments of deep human connection.

If I flip through the mental photo album of my career, I find that I am no exception to the rule. The high-water marks in my work life are not particularly big, public, or lucrative. They are vivid moments, colored by hard work, a sense of progress, and a thick set of connections.

George Vaillant, who directed the Harvard Study of Adult Development for over three decades, concluded similarly when he wrote, "Happiness equals love. Full stop."[11] After leading the longest study of adult life for decades, Vaillant's observations boil down into a few powerful, pithy words on connection. Every team leader I know wants their team to work hard and feel a sense of progress and fulfillment from the effort. Meaningful connection across the team sets the stage for work that may just show up as someone's high-water mark when they reflect on their career memories.

CONCLUSION

The Alchemy of You

"Be the thermostat, not the thermometer."

I've been thinking about this classic leadership advice while writing this book. If you've not encountered this guidance, let me explain its intended use first. Some leaders, often ineffective ones, operate like a thermometer: if things are tense and hot, they are stressed and anxious. Everyone on the team knows it. They unconsciously reflect the temperature of the moment, like a thermometer. At the end of a book on leading high-performance teams, I don't need to unpack why this is far from ideal! A thermostat, by contrast, sets the temperature. If things are running hot, a leader can exert a calming influence, stabilizing the team with vision and reassurance. If things are running cold, the leader can motivate the team by revisiting the team's "why" or turning up the volume on recognition. The leader who sets and maintains the optimal temperature is far more likely to help the team and organization outperform consistently.

Here's the catch: if you want to lead your team to greatness using the Alchemy of Talent, operating as a thermostat is insufficient. I know, I know . . . it sounds great to be the thermostat compared to the thermometer,[1] but let's return to the preface of this book to see why it still isn't enough.

I opened this book with a discussion of how volatility and uncertainty are hallmarks of work life in the 21st century. Disruption is the only constant. High-performance teams have razor-sharp skills and a deep capacity for productivity. They also must be extremely agile to function in the new normal of continuous, rapid change. The thermostat, unfortunately, can be clunky and flat-footed rather than agile and dynamic.

For a thermostat to function well, it needs a target temperature. Think of this as a clear, defined goal that stays generally constant. To achieve this goal, the thermostat has three modes: heat, cool, and off. These are analogous to the thermostat leader's tools: they are fixed and very well-known. If the goal is to maintain a temperature of seventy degrees Fahrenheit, the thermostat leader will efficiently apply either heating or cooling to achieve the desired target and then move to off when the target is attained.

In the 21st-century world of work, we need a leader that can go far beyond this.

Continuous disruption necessitates cultivating a set of skills that are more dynamic than thermostat leadership. The leader that can fully apply the Alchemy of Talent has to work within shifting or unclear goals, develop new skills as macro conditions change our work context, and embrace a learning stance that moves the ego aside so they can take healthy risks and fail without an identity crisis. When coaching executive leaders I frequently emphasize these leadership skills to help my clients go beyond the thermostat and optimize the Alchemy of Talent.

Humility

Volatility and uncertainty require you to see yourself with clarity and accept that you will make mistakes. Keen self-awareness—the first part of humility—is a must for leaders to understand what they are bringing into every situation. This is everything from your own inherent and acquired traits, which contribute to your point of view on life and work (see Chapter 1), to clarity on your strengths and weaknesses, so you can hire a team that offsets what you've brought to work.

The second part of humility is about the ego. As a leader, much is asked of you. It's easy to start thinking through the ego, which centers a heroic version of you as the driver for every element of the team's success. The pressures of leadership can spotlight the ego, but adaptive leaders know that they have to sideline the ego to succeed. In the future of work, you will be asked to lead with shifting goals in unfamiliar contexts, making some amount of failure inevitable. This failure risk can be paralyzing for leaders that haven't embraced humility because they believe any failure at work means *they are a failure*, rather than simply viewing the experience as a failure at a task or challenge.

Sense-Making

For a 21st-century leader to go beyond the thermostat we need to cultivate situational awareness. This is the skill of asking why and applying empathy. Asking why can help a leader succeed when goals are unclear or shifting. Understanding the root cause is critical to sense-making in times of uncertainty. Adept leaders can also help their teams sense-make by leading discussions that go beyond task execution to think dynamically about the macro and micro conditions that are contributing to the team's experience.

Empathy is the skill of sitting in other people's thoughts or feelings. Like any skill, it can be cultivated and improved with practice. My clients often find this surprising but the neuroscience research is clear here.[2] With focused effort leaders can get better at truly understanding how other people think and feel. When we lead complex teams, we have the blessing of diverse experiences, skills, and perspectives in our squad! This can be a superpower . . . if the leader has the empathy to connect across meaningful differences and maintain cohesion during volatility. Change is hard on teams, and every member of the team may feel and think differently about a moment of change. Leading a complex team today requires the empathy to nimbly adapt your leadership to bring the best out of people who may think and feel differently than you do.

Seeking Friction

Antifragile things improve from shock or friction. In the midst of change fatigue and general overwhelm, I frequently remind my clients that adaptive leaders are antifragile. The numerous disruptions in the world of work can be experienced as simple hardship, or they can be productive friction. The differentiator is you. Humility and empathy contribute to creating dynamic leadership where you can harness friction to spin the flywheel of agility and learning.

There's evidence that we progressively avoid friction as we age. Young people have a greater tolerance for clashing perspectives and ways of being. As we age, we often seek comfort through commonality, both in our personal lives and at work. The Alchemy of Talent requires friction, for your team and you. I coach leaders to seek friction, even if they are highly successful and widely lauded for their brilliance and impact. In fact, these are the leaders most at risk of avoiding friction and missing out on antifragility. The world is telling them that they have arrived. Without humility and empathy to push back on this false, fixed mindset, leaders can unknowingly rob themselves of powerful transformation by gravitating toward echo chambers.

Retrospectives

In Chapter 3 of this book, I talked about the power of rituals for increasing belonging on a team. Leaders also need rituals in their own lives that foster agility. Ritualizing retrospectives is a must for leaders navigating volatility and change. Retrospectives are reflection exercises designed to foster awareness and learning. There are countless models for retrospectives which are easily accessible online. I encourage leaders to find a model that works well for their style and philosophy.

In general, retrospectives involve asking four questions: What happened? What went well? What didn't go well? What can I learn? Leaders should use retrospectives with their teams on a regular basis, particularly after a major milestone in a project.

The same cadence can be applied to your own life as a leader. On a weekly or monthly basis, commit to a ten-minute personal reflection of your leadership. What were some key moments for you and your team in this last period? What have you been doing well? What hasn't gone well? What can you learn, and how can you adapt to be more successful? Retrospectives really start to fly when supercharged with humility and empathy. Asking why, being open to failure, and thinking from other people's perspectives can turn a ritual of reflection into high-impact learning. The leader who embraces friction can also check in with people who are different from themselves to enhance a retrospective. The dissonance from their view may just be the catalyst you need to say, "Aha!"

Getting Better

In a time of overwhelm and change fatigue, I want to be cautious and recognize that this list of skills can feel onerous. But I find that leaders are already working extremely hard to adapt and succeed at work. This is a list of skills that isn't about working harder, but differently. Think of these four skills as your "fundamentals of agility" that allow you to lead more fluidly in the 21st century. If disruption is the only constant, our leadership fundamentals need to be purpose-built for this ethos. Part of the overwhelm and change fatigue we feel is because many of us are still using leadership fundamentals from a previous era. Working extremely hard to be the best thermostat you can be is exhausting, especially when it leaves you short of what the future of work demands. Take heart . . . it gets better! This is a message we all need to hear these days.

> *It gets better, if we have the*
> *agility to allow it to get better.*

Let's return to a metaphor to see how going "beyond the thermostat" actually makes things easier for leaders in the 21st century.

Think back to the story in the preface of this book. You are leading a team on a hike through the mountains. You reach a chasm with no bridge. You have the benefit of a complex team, and your location is filled with helpful resources. Fog is rolling in, and visibility is low. In the preface, I used this story to emphasize the difference between management and leadership during times of volatility and change. The story pointed to the need to not only build a great bridge but to inspire your team to follow you across that bridge. A competent thermostat leader can accomplish both of these tasks. They can manage the execution roadmap to get the bridge built efficiently while also modulating emotionally to inspire the team to follow them across the bridge. Whew! *Puff, puff, puff* . . . doable . . . but exhausting.

The agile leader may approach this entire situation differently. Instead of thinking about this story as bridge-building and followership, what if the leader turned to their skilled, complex team and said, "How do we proceed?" It may turn out that there is an expert hang

glider in the group. Or someone may have brought enough rope to use rappelling and climbing as a way to move forward. Or someone may know how to make a hot air balloon! Some, or many of these solutions, may be easier and more efficient than building a bridge.* Humility and empathy can increase this kind of pivot moment in your leadership journey. Yes, times are tough. But, it does get better. The Alchemy of You is just around the corner, and I cannot wait to journey with you.

---

* A special note of gratitude to the VMware DEI and Talent Acquisition team for introducing me to this powerful metaphor for leadership.

NOTES

Preface

1   Gallup, "State of the Global Workplace Report,"
    Gallup, 2023, https://www.gallup.com/
    workplace/349484/state-of-the-global-workplace.
    aspx.
2   Airspeed, "2 out of 3 Execs Believe Their Workers
    Will Quit Because They Feel Disconnected, and
    It's the #1 Reason Workers Say They'll Leave,"
    Airspeed, September 13, 2022, https://www.
    getairspeed.com/blog/execs-believe-workers-quit-
    because-they-feel-disconnected-the-1-reason-
    workers-say-theyll-leave/.
3   Jean M Twenge, *Generations* (Simon and Schuster,
    2023).

Introduction

1   Turner, Jordan. "What Will HR Focus on in 2023?"
    Gartner, 4 Oct. 2022, www.gartner.com/en/articles/
    what-will-hr-focus-on-in-2023.

Chapter 1

1   Nassim Nicholas Taleb, *Antifragile: Things That Gain from Disorder* (New York: Random House, 2016), 3.

2   Dame Vivian Hunt, Dennis Layton, and Sara Prince, "Why Diversity Matters," McKinsey & Company, January 1, 2015, https://www.mckinsey.com/capabilities/people-and-organizational-performance/our-insights/why-diversity-matters.

3   Bernardo M. Ferdman and Barbara Deane, *Diversity at Work the Practice of Inclusion* (San Francisco, California Wiley, 2014).

4   David A. Harrison and Katherine J. Klein, "What's the Difference? Diversity Constructs as Separation, Variety, or Disparity in Organizations," *Academy of Management Review* 32, no. 4 (October 2007): 1199–1228, https://doi.org/10.5465/amr.2007.26586096.

5   Sheen S. Levine et al., "Ethnic Diversity Deflates Price Bubbles," *Proceedings of the National Academy of Sciences* 111, no. 52 (November 17, 2014): 18524–29, https://doi.org/10.1073/pnas.1407301111.

Chapter 2

1   Henrik Bresman and Amy Edmondson, "Research: To Excel, Diverse Teams Need Psychological Safety," *Harvard Business Review,* March 17, 2022, https://hbr.org/2022/03/research-to-excel-diverse-teams-need-psychological-safety.

2   Amy Edmondson, "Psychological Safety and Learning Behavior in Work Teams," *Administrative Science Quarterly* 44, no. 2 (June 1999): 350–83, https://doi.org/10.2307/2666999.

3   Edgar H. Schein and Warren G. Bennis, *Personal and Organizational Change through Group Methods: The Laboratory Approach* (New York: John Wiley, 1967).

4   Amy Edmondson, "Psychological Safety and Learning Behavior in Work Teams," *Administrative Science Quarterly* 44, no. 2 (June 1999): 350–83, https://doi.org/10.2307/2666999.

5   Timothy R. Clark, *The 4 Stages of Psychological Safety: Defining the Path to Inclusion and Innovation* (Oakland, CA: Berrett-Koehler Publishers, Inc., 2020).

6   Michael Schneider, "Google Spent 2 Years Studying 180 Teams. The Most Successful Ones Shared These 5 Traits," Inc.com (July 19, 2017): https://www.inc.com/michael-schneider/google-thought-they-knew-how-to-create-the-perfect.html.

7   Henrik Bresman and Amy Edmondson, "Research: To Excel, Diverse Teams Need Psychological Safety," *Harvard Business Review*, March 17, 2022, https://hbr.org/2022/03/research-to-excel-diverse-teams-need-psychological-safety.

Chapter 3

1   Bernie Wong and Kelly Greenwood, "The Future of Mental Health at Work Is Safety, Community, and a Healthy Organizational Culture," *Harvard Business Review*, October 10, 2023, https://hbr.org/2023/10/the-future-of-mental-health-at-work-is-safety-community-and-a-healthy-organizational-culture.

2   Gallup, "The Wellbeing-Engagement Paradox of 2020," Gallup.com, March 13, 2021, https://www.gallup.com/workplace/336941/wellbeing-engagement-paradox-2020.aspx.

3   Coqual, "Coqual - Diversity, Equity & Inclusion | Formerly Center for Talent Innovation," Coqual, n.d., https://coqual.org/.

4   Naomi I. Eisenberger, "The Neural Bases of Social Pain," *Psychosomatic Medicine* 74, no. 2 (2012): 126–35, https://doi.org/10.1097/psy.0b013e3182464dd1.

5   Aaron De Smet et al., "How Companies Can Turn
     the Great Resignation into the Great Attraction |
     McKinsey," McKinsey, September 8, 2021, https://
     www.mckinsey.com/capabilities/people-and-
     organizational-performance/our-insights/great-
     attrition-or-great-attraction-the-choice-is-yours#/.
6   BetterUp, "The Value of Belonging at Work:
     The Business Case for Investing in Workplace
     Inclusion," grow.betterup.com, November 4,
     2019, https://grow.betterup.com/resources/
     the-value-of-belonging-at-work-the-business-
     case-for-investing-in-workplace-inclusion/
     watch.
7   Gallup and Workhuman, "Empowering Workplace
     Culture Through Recognition," Gallup, 2024.
     https://www.gallup.com/analytics/472658/
     workplace-recognition-research.aspx.
8   Adrian Robert Gostick and Chester Elton, *The
     Carrot Principle: How the Best Managers Use
     Recognition to Engage Their People, Retain Talent, and
     Accelerate Performance* (New York, NY: Free Press,
     2009).

Chapter 4

1   Abhishek Sharma, "Want Engaged Employees? Encourage Human Resource and Enhance Organizational Connectedness," *Australian Journal of Business and Management Research* 6, no. 1 (April 2021): 1–12, https://doi.org/10.52283/nswrca. ajbmr.hxnp5021.

2   Naz Beheshti, "10 Timely Statistics about the Connection between Employee Engagement and Wellness," *Forbes*, January 16, 2019, https://www. forbes.com/sites/nazbeheshti/2019/01/16/10- timely-statistics-about-the-connection- between-employee-engagement-and- wellness/?sh=147bbeeb22a0.

3   George E. Vaillant, *Triumphs of Experience: The Men of the Harvard Grant Study* (Cambridge: The Belknap Press Of Harvard University Press, 2015).

4   Gallup Inc, "The Tenth Element of Great Managing," Gallup.com, February 14, 2008, https:// news.gallup.com/businessjournal/104197/Tenth- Element-Great-Managing.aspx.

5   Gallup Inc, "The Tenth Element of Great Managing," Gallup.com, February 14, 2008, https:// news.gallup.com/businessjournal/104197/Tenth- Element-Great-Managing.aspx.

6   Daniel Coyle, *The Culture Code* (Random House UK, 2019).

7   Jessica R. Methot and Michael S. Cole,
      "Unpacking the Microdynamics of Multiplex
      Peer Developmental Relationships: A Mutuality
      Perspective," *Journal of Management* 49, no. 2
      (December 23, 2021): 014920632110484, https://
      doi.org/10.1177/01492063211048437.

8   Daniel Coyle, "How Showing Vulnerability Helps
      Build a Stronger Team," Ideas. TED, February
      20, 2018, https://ideas.ted.com/how-showing-
      vulnerability-helps-build-a-stronger-team/.

9   Norton, Michael I., Daniel Mochon, and Dan Ariely,
      "The 'IKEA effect': When labor leads to love," *SSRN
      Electronic Journal* (2011), https://doi.org/10.2139/
      ssrn.1777100.

10   Jacob Morgan, *Leading with Vulnerability: Unlock
      your Greatest Superpower to Transform Yourself, Your
      Team, and Your Organization* (Hoboken, NJ: Wiley
      Press, 2023).

11   George E. Valliant, "Yes, I Stand by My
      Words, 'Happiness Equals Love—Full Stop,'"
      Positive Psychology News, July 16, 2009,
      https://positivepsychologynews.com/news/
      george-vaillant/200907163163.

Conclusion

1   Chris Argyris, *Teaching Smart People How to Learn* (Boston, MA: Harvard Business Press, 2008).

2   Jamil Zaki, *The War for Kindness: Building Empathy in a Fractured World* (Crown Publishing Group, 2019).

ACKNOWLEDGMENTS

To Katie, for foregoing weekends with me so I could write this book, and for fiercely claiming them back as soon as I was done.

To the tailwinds: the rest of my family were instrumental to my momentum, through the weeks and months of drafting and revisions. So much love to Mira, Savi, Mom, Dad, Sumi, and Sunil for cheering me on and finding moments along the way to celebrate the milestones.

To the besties: my closest friends offered conversation and companionship that made the otherwise lonely process of writing feel bearable and, at times, quite fun. Love and gratitude to my crew: Art, Ann Marie, Casey, Carl, Byron, Brian, Leah, Theresa, Emily, and Marty (with whom I keep chatting, even if he is no longer here).

To my co-conspirator extraordinaire, Mikaela. Thank you for constantly reminding me of "the why," holding me accountable to the deadlines, and giving me space to occasionally freak out. You were a catalyst in making this book happen.

To the mentors and supervisors who taught me so much about leading teams. Too many to name here, but I am so lucky to have had tremendous "wise elders" in my career who helped me do the best work of my life. A book about leading teams to greatness would never have crossed my mind or heart if I didn't have the inspiration of your leadership.

ABOUT THE AUTHOR

Dr. Vijay Pendakur is principal and founder of Vijay Pendakur Consulting. A true multi-sector organizational leader, Pendakur has held senior roles at four companies: Salesforce, Dropbox, VMware, and Zynga. He has also served as the Robert W. and Elizabeth C. Staley Dean of Students at Cornell University. In his time at the largest Ivy League institution, he was named Presidential Advisor for Diversity and Equity as part of a new approach to campus-wide transformation.

His 2016 book *Closing the Opportunity Gap* represents one of the few book-length works on how to graduate underserved college students and is still used by campus leaders today to inform strategy. Pendakur has served as an advisor to the Chief Diversity Officer of the National

Institutes of Health, and he serves on the institute teaching faculty of the Race and Equity Center at the University of Southern California. Pendakur is a board advisor for Ezra Coaching and Enterprise Ireland.

When he's not working, he's strumming guitars, sampling single malts, and enjoying the creeks and trails around Austin with his wife and daughters.